SECONDARY EDUCATION IN A CHANGING WORLD

Series editors: Barry M. Franklin and Gary McCulloch

Published by Palgrave Macmillan:

The Comprehensive Public High School: Historical Perspectives
By Geoffrey Sherington and Craig Campbell
(2006)

Cyril Norwood and the Ideal of Secondary Education
By Gary McCulloch
(2007)

The Death of the Comprehensive High School?:
Historical, Contemporary, and Comparative Perspectives
Edited by Barry M. Franklin and Gary McCulloch
(2007)

The Emergence of Holocaust Education in American Schools
By Thomas D. Fallace
(2008)

The Standardization of American Schooling:
Linking Secondary and Higher Education, 1870–1910
By Marc A. VanOverbeke
(2008)

Education and Social Integration:
Comprehensive Schooling in Europe
By Susanne Wiborg
(2009)

Reforming New Zealand Secondary Education:
The Picot Report and the Road to Radical Reform
By Roger Openshaw
(2009)

Inciting Change in Secondary English Language Programs:
The Case of Cherry High School
By Marilee Coles-Ritchie
(2009)

Curriculum, Community, and Urban School Reform
By Barry M. Franklin
(2010)

Girls' Secondary Education in the Western World:
From the 18th to the 20th Century
Edited by James C. Albisetti, Joyce Goodman, and Rebecca Rogers
(2010)

Race-Class Relations and Integration in Secondary Education:
The Case of Miller High
By Caroline Eick
(2010)

Teaching Harry Potter: The Power of Imagination in
Multicultural Classrooms
By Catherine L. Belcher and Becky Herr Stephenson
(2011)

The Invention of the Secondary Curriculum
By John White
(2011)

Secondary STEM Educational Reform
Edited by Carla C. Johnson
(2011)

New Labour and Secondary Education, 1994–2010
By Clyde Chitty
(2013)

New Labour and Secondary Education, 1994–2010

Clyde Chitty

palgrave
macmillan

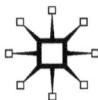

NEW LABOUR AND SECONDARY EDUCATION, 1994–2010
Copyright © Clyde Chitty, 2013.
Softcover reprint of the hardcover 1st edition 2013 978-0-230-34061-9
All rights reserved.

First published in 2013 by
PALGRAVE MACMILLAN®
in the United States—a division of St. Martin's Press LLC,
175 Fifth Avenue, New York, NY 10010.

Where this book is distributed in the UK, Europe and the rest of the world, this is by Palgrave Macmillan, a division of Macmillan Publishers Limited, registered in England, company number 785998, of Houndmills, Basingstoke, Hampshire RG21 6XS.

Palgrave Macmillan is the global academic imprint of the above companies and has companies and representatives throughout the world.

Palgrave® and Macmillan® are registered trademarks in the United States, the United Kingdom, Europe and other countries.

ISBN 978-1-349-34318-8   ISBN 978-1-137-07632-8 (eBook)
DOI 10.1057/9781137076328

Library of Congress Cataloging-in-Publication Data
Chitty, Clyde.
    New labour and secondary education, 1994–2010 / Clyde Chitty.
        pages cm.—(Secondary education in a changing world)

    1. Education, Secondary—Great Britain. 2. Labour Party (Great Britain)—Platforms. I. Title.
LA635.C55 2013
373.41—dc23   2012043582

A catalogue record of the book is available from the British Library.

Design by Newgen Imaging Systems (P) Ltd., Chennai, India.

First edition: May 2013

10 9 8 7 6 5 4 3 2 1

Transferred to Digital Printing in 2013

Contents

Series Editors' Foreword	vii
Acknowledgments	xi
List of Secretaries of State for Education, 1964–2010	xiii
List of Shadow Education Ministers, 1979–1997	xv
1 Introduction	1
2 The Origins of Political Parties in Britain: Consensus or Conflict? The Situation in Britain Today	7
3 Labour Education Policy, 1944–1994: 50 Years of Missed Opportunities and Uneasy Compromises	31
4 A Change of Direction: The Origins of New Labour's Education Philosophy	57
5 Choice, Diversity, and Selection: The Steady Abandonment of the Comprehensive Ideal, 1997–2007	79
6 The Privatization of Education	107
7 The Erosion of the National Curriculum	129
8 International Perspectives	151
9 Conclusion	167
References	169
Index	179

Series Editors' Foreword

Among the educational issues affecting policy makers, public officials, and citizens in modern, democratic, and industrial societies, none has been more contentious than the role of secondary schooling. In establishing the Secondary Education in a Changing World series with Palgrave Macmillan, our intent is to provide a venue for scholars in different national settings to explore critical and controversial issues surrounding secondary education. We envision our series as a place for the airing and resolution of these controversial issues.

More than a century has elapsed since Emile Durkheim argued the importance of studying secondary education as a unity, rather than in relation to the wide range of subjects and the division of pedagogical labor of which it was composed. Only thus, he insisted, would it be possible to have the ends and aims of secondary education constantly in view. The failure to do so accounted for a great deal of difficulty that secondary education faced. First, it meant that secondary education was "intellectually disoriented," between "a past which is dying and a future which is still undecided," and, as a result, "lacks the vigor and vitality which it once possessed" (Durkheim 1938/1977, p. 8). Second, the institutions of secondary education were not understood adequately in relation to their past, which was "the soil which nourished them and gave them their present meaning, and apart from which they cannot be examined without a great deal of impoverishment and distortion" (p. 10). And third, it was difficult for secondary school teachers, who were responsible for putting policy reforms into practice, to understand their nature and the problems and issues that prompted them.

In the early decades of the twenty-first century, Durkheim's strictures still have resonance. The intellectual disorientation of secondary education is more evident than ever as it is caught up in successive waves of policy changes. The connections between the present and the past have become increasingly hard to trace and untangle. Moreover, the distance between policy makers on the one hand and the practitioners on the other has rarely seemed as immense as it is today. The key mission of the current series of books is, in the spirit of Durkheim, to address these underlying dilemmas of secondary education and to play a part in resolving them.

Clyde Chitty's *New Labour and Secondary Education, 1994–2010* explores New Labour's policy toward secondary education in Britain from the election of Tony Blair as leader of the Labour Party in 1994 until the defeat of Gordon Brown's Labour government in 2010. His book tells the story of the accession of New Labour to power in 1997, the legislative and policy victories and defeats over the next 13 years, and New Labour's defeat in the general election of 2010. In part the book is descriptive and explores the period in which New Labour came to power and its years of government. Reflecting the Third Way philosophy espoused by Anthony Giddens in the United Kingdom and Bill Clinton in the United States, New Labour sought to articulate a new pattern of governance for the globalized world of the twenty-first century. What Blair and his party hoped to achieve was to redefine the role of the state and to establish a new relationship between citizenship rights and state responsibility that challenged the existing Right and Left governing modes of twentieth-century Britain. Key to its governing philosophy was the attempt to go beyond traditional progressive and conservative ideas and policies in favor of a new brand of politics that, rather than splitting existing Left-Right differences, sought a set of relations with a common sphere where both views could find a home. At one level, the book is a description of the various stages in the 13 years of New Labour's control. Beyond that, however, it is a powerful analysis of what that rule meant to the administration of the British state generally and to the Third Way governance in particular.

At the heart of Chitty's volume is a discussion of New Labour's continuation of the policy agenda promoted by the previous Conservative government. Having said that, however, it is important to note that New Labor did embark on its own initiatives. The party did not continue its longstanding support of the comprehensive school. By the time Gordon Brown assumed the party's leadership, New Labor was promoting approximately 20 alternatives to the traditional comprehensive school. A particularly unique feature of New Labour's educational agenda was the promotion of privatization that reversed the commitment, itself often somewhat half-hearted, of Labor to the comprehensive school. In doing so, New Labor embraced the privatization movement that was gaining headway in the globalized world of the twenty-first century.

As the fourteenth volume in our series, Chitty's book brings together many of the arguments that were raised in earlier volumes about the expansion and globalization of secondary education at the end of the twentieth and beginning of the twenty-first centuries. It offers the foundation for additional volumes that might explore a number of these emerging trends in educational provision for secondary youth as well as suggests new areas of inquiry for the series as we extend the focus more deliberately beyond the United States and United Kingdom.

BARRY M. FRANKLIN
GARY MCCULLOCH
Series Coeditors

Acknowledgments

My thanks are due to all my colleagues and students, both past and present, at Goldsmiths College and at the Institute of Education, who have never been reluctant to take issue with many of the views expressed in this book, and to put forward alternative perspectives of their own. I owe a special debt of gratitude to my friend and colleague Professor Gary McCulloch, joint editor of the series of which this book forms a part, for reading some of the chapters in draft form, and for all his constructive suggestions and sound advice. And my warmest thanks go to Chi, for all his help with the preparation of the manuscript in its final form.

Secretaries of State for Education, 1964–2010

Quintin Hogg	April 1964–October 1964
Michael Stewart	October 1964–January 1965
Anthony Crosland	January 1965–August 1967
Patrick Gordon-Walker	August 1967–April 1968
Edward Short	April 1968–June 1970
Margaret Thatcher	June 1970–March 1974
Reginald Prentice	March 1974–June 1975
Fred Mulley	June 1975–September 1976
Shirley Williams	September 1976–May 1979
Mark Carlisle	May 1979–September 1981
Keith Joseph	September 1981–May 1986
Kenneth Baker	May 1986–July 1989
John MacGregor	July 1989–November 1990
Kenneth Clarke	November 1990–April 1992
John Patten	April 1992–July 1994
Gillian Shephard	July 1994–May 1997
David Blunkett	May 1997–June 2001
Estelle Morris	June 2001–October 2002
Charles Clarke	October 2002–December 2004
Ruth Kelly	December 2004–May 2006
Alan Johnson	May 2006–June 2007
Ed Balls	June 2007–May 2010

Shadow Education Ministers, 1979–1997

Neil Kinnock	1979–1983
Giles Radice	1983–1987
Jack Straw	1987–1992
Ann Taylor	1992–1994
David Blunkett	1994–1997*

*David Blunkett went on to become Tony Blair's first Education Secretary, from 1997 to 2001

Chapter 1

Introduction

It is hoped that this book will stand on its own as a detailed study of New Labour's policy toward secondary education in Britain, starting from Tony Blair's election as leader of the Labour Party in July 1994, to the defeat of Gordon Brown's Labour government in the general election of May 2010. But it can also be seen as a sort of sequel to an earlier book I have written under the title *Towards a New Education System: The Victory of the New Right?* published in 1989 (Chitty, 1989a). Based on research for a University of London doctorate, this was a study of the politics of education in England and Wales from 1976 to 1988, and, bearing in mind that much of the so-called education establishment was united in its opposition to the market-driven proposals in the Conservative government's 1988 Education Reform Act, the book ended on a fairly optimistic and upbeat note: "The question mark in the title of this book remains firmly in place, and will not easily be dislodged" (p. 227). It now seems clear to me that that optimism was somewhat misplaced. One of the purposes of this present book is to show how so many aspects of the education agenda of Margaret Thatcher's government were continued, and expanded upon, by all the governments (both Conservative and New Labour) that followed. It will, in fact, be argued that the postwar education settlement that was dismantled at the end of the 1980s remains in pieces today, as we come to terms with living in a post–welfare society. It is perhaps necessary to explain why we shall be using the term *New* Labour, rather than Labour, to describe the party that came to power in May 1997. As we shall see in chapter 4, it was at the time of the 1994 Labour Party conference that Tony Blair decided that it was essential to rename the party in order to emphasize a complete break with the past. (He had, in fact, been elected leader just three months earlier, in July). And it was his new press spokesperson, Alastair Campbell, who invented the phrase "New Labour, New Britain," as the slogan for the conference. Some of those in the higher echelons of the party were uneasy about the change, and preferred to talk in terms of "new Labour," with *no* capital N for the word "new"; but Blair insisted that only by renaming the party as "New Labour," could they hope to convince other people, particularly commentators in the often hostile media, that this new party was *not* the old Labour Party.

In his 2010 political memoir, *A Journey*, Tony Blair explained that this was all part of the process of espousing a "Third Way" in British politics. This was the title of a book by LSE (London School of Economics) sociologist Anthony Giddens, published in 1998 (Giddens, 1998a), following up the themes pursued in an earlier book, published in 1994, and significantly titled *Beyond Left and Right* (Giddens, 1994). But Blair has also been anxious to stress the debt he owes to American president Bill Clinton (1993–1997; 1997–2001) in formulating a new and distinctive political philosophy:

> Bill Clinton was the most formidable politician I had ever encountered. And yet his very expertise and extraordinary capacity at the business of politics obscured the fact that he was also a brilliant thinker, with a clear and thought-through political philosophy and programme.... The Third Way philosophy that we both espoused was not a clever splitting of the difference between Right and Left. Neither was it simply lowest common denominator populism. It was a genuine, coherent and actually successful attempt to redefine progressive politics in our countries: to liberate it from outdated ideology; to apply its values anew in a new world; to reform the role of government and of the state; and to create a modern relationship between the responsibilities of the citizen and those of society—a hand *up*, not a hand *out* on welfare, opportunity and responsibility, as the basis of a strong society It was a way of moving *beyond* the "small-state," "no role for society" ideology of the Republicans and the Conservatives; and the "big-state," anti-enterprise ideology of the traditional Democratic base. It was we who should be the good economic managers; the people who understood concern about crime; the ones that got aspiration, and actually empathized with it. (Blair, 2010, pp. 321–32)

Let me stress at the outset that I am well aware of the doubts and misgivings that are often expressed about the *value* of writing contemporary history. It is certainly true that the process of writing about the *very recent* past can well be a frustrating experience, in that the events described can never have a real "end point," and all the judgments one makes have to be transitory and provisional. Professor Andrew Gamble, who has written many acclaimed books and articles analyzing postwar British politics, has argued that "there are few things more difficult than trying to make sense of contemporary political events, and the direction in which they are moving" (Gamble, 1988, p. x). Gamble stresses that the "confident judgments and assertions" one is often tempted to make can all too easily be nullified by unforeseen happenings. And the Marxist historian Eric Hobsbawm has gone so far as to suggest that contemporary events are not really a proper subject for the historian. In an essay on the formation of British working-class culture, written in 1979, he argued that "like Britain itself, anchored in the nineteenth century, the British working class is in danger of losing its bearings. But its present situation and prospects are a subject for the reporter and the sociologist. They are not yet a proper subject for the historian" (Hobsbawm, 1984, p. 193).

That said, there are those who defend the practice of attempting to say what *can* be said about recent and contemporary events, provided one accepts that the writing of all history is as much about explanation as it is about judgment. In his 1977 biography of Ramsay MacDonald, Professor David Marquand argues that "the historian is not a kind of celestial chief justice, sentencing the guilty and setting free the innocent. He (sic) is always part of the process he describes, and his judgements can never be more than provisional" (Marquand, 1977, p. 791). And in his latest book, *Distilling the Frenzy: Writing the History of One's Own Times*, Peter Hennessy, one of United Kingdom's leading contemporary historians, makes the case for exploring the major themes of one's own times, and lists the things that motivate him as a historian of the present: "The special curiosity attached to shared, lived moments, events, transformations, air breathed, noises heard; the powerful desire to make sense of your own time and to place configurations upon it, while avoiding excessive patterning, mono-causal explanations, or the condescending and patronising urge to tell the veterans how they should have felt, if only they had thought about it harder" (Hennessy, 2012, p. 20).

The Structure of the Book

Chapter 2 provides the context for much that is to follow, by offering a brief overview of the period from 1945 to 2010: from the period when most of Britain's governing class shared a political philosophy that might be called "Keynesian Social Democracy" to the situation today when much of social policy is governed by a set of market state priorities. There is an examination of the history of the three main political parties in Britain, or, more specifically, in England, to see how they have responded to the social and economic pressures of the day. It is argued that the last 20 years have witnessed the triumph of a new right-wing consensus that rejects most of the guiding principles of the postwar "welfare capitalist consensus."

Chapter 3 concentrates on the education policy of the Labour Party from the 1944 Education Act to the election of Tony Blair as party leader in July 1994. It argues that, looked at from a radical, progressive perspective, it was a period of "missed opportunities and uneasy compromises," in that the party was never able to determine what it actually meant by a policy of "secondary education for all," and it was also generally ambivalent in its attitude toward comprehensive education. By contrast, the last administration of Margaret Thatcher (1987–1990) offered a coherent ideological approach to the structure of the education system, which had the effect of throwing the Labour Party on the defensive. Having examined the Thatcher legacy, chapter 4 looks at the change of direction in Labour education policy that was part of Tony Blair's attempt to change the nature of the party. This involved a refusal to make a clear and unequivocal commitment to the comprehensive principle at the secondary stage and a determination to continue with the Major administration's emphasis on standards and accountability.

Chapter 5 examines the education priorities of the New Labour governments from 1997 to 2010, which involved a concern to promote choice and diversity at the secondary level and to secure the creation of many new types of schools. To raise educational standards in a changing global community, it was thought to be necessary to move *beyond* the comprehensive era, while retaining the rhetoric of "inclusion" and "equality of opportunity." New Labour had to be seen as the party which understood the concerns of the aspiring middle class.

One of the dominant themes of education policy since at least the 1980s has been an emphasis on the merits of privatization, and this is the subject of chapter 6. It is stressed in this chapter that we are not talking about a one-dimensional phenomenon, and an attempt is made to understand some of its component parts, including the Academies Programme initiated in 2000; the Private Finance Initiative launched in the early 1990s; and the development of the so-called edu-market, involving the growth of large groups of "chains" running both primary and secondary schools, often with links abroad. Chapter 7 is concerned with the steady abandonment of the National Curriculum which was very much the brainchild of Kenneth Baker, and introduced as part of the 1988 Education Reform Act. Its erosion has been particularly pronounced at Key Stage Four, the stage concerned with the education of 14- to 16-year-old students, where the original framework has been effectively reduced to a limited "core" of the main traditional subjects. This chapter also deals with the debate over an effective qualifications system for 14- to 19-year-olds, concentrating on New Labour's initial rejection of the 2004 Tomlinson Report, advocating a unified framework of 14–19 curriculum and qualifications.

Chapter 8 views recent education developments in England in the context of the international scene, focusing particularly on trends in America, Australia, New Zealand, and Scandinavia. It seems to be the case that the future of the comprehensive high school is in doubt in many other parts of the world.

The final chapter, chapter 9, attempts to analyze, and draw conclusions from, the preoccupations and themes that have characterized New Labour education policy from 1994 to 2010.

Chapter 2

The Origins of Political Parties in Britain: Consensus or Conflict? The Situation in Britain Today

There are currently three main parties in British politics—the Conservative Party, the Labour Party and the Liberal Democrats—and since the general election of May 2010, the country has had a coalition government comprising two of these parties: the Conservatives led by David Cameron and the Liberal Democrats led by Nick Clegg. As the leader of the largest party in the House of Commons, with the Conservatives having 306 seats in May 2010, David Cameron is the prime minister, with Nick Clegg acting as his deputy.

As the role of the Crown diminished and that of parliament became more powerful in the eighteenth and nineteenth centuries, it proved necessary to foster the growth of political parties so that the process of governing, and of carrying on the business of opposition, could be organized in a fairly systematic way. Without a degree of party discipline it would be quite impossible, even for a government that had secured widespread electoral support, to be certain of getting all its legislation through the House of Commons and the House of Lords. When Robert Peel's Conservative government decided in 1846 to repeal the Corn Laws, making bread cheaper and, or so it was hoped, within the purchasing power of the poor by the complete removal of import duties on grain, the effect was also to alienate the diehard protectionists in the Conservative Party; and it was the rising politician Benjamin Disraeli who made a famous speech in the House of Commons in January 1846 articulating the view that loyalty to party must always be paramount:

> Let men stand by the principle by which they rise, right or wrong. I make no exception.... Do not, because you see a great personage giving up his opinions—do not cheer him on.... Above all, maintain the line of demarcation between parties, for it is only by maintaining the independence and integrity of party that you can maintain the integrity of public men—and the power and influence of Parliament itself. (Quoted in Blake, 1966, p. 227)

Even so, and despite Disraeli's strong warning, it has always been true that the main political parties at Westminster are themselves virtual coalitions, with the ministers and MPs who adopt a particular party label often disagreeing among themselves about key aspects of party policy. Indeed, there have been interesting occasions when politicians from opposing parties have campaigned together in support of a particular cause. The meetings leading up to the referendum on Britain's membership of the European Economic Community (or Common Market), held on June 5, 1975, involved some surprising, if only temporary, alliances between erstwhile political "enemies." Rallies held by the Coalition for Europe were addressed by Edward Heath, until February 1975—when he was replaced by Margaret Thatcher—leader of the Conservative Party; Jeremy Thorpe, the leader of the Liberal Party; and Roy Jenkins, until September 1976 home secretary in the Labour government. Prominent politicians campaigning for withdrawal from the EEC included three left-wing secretaries of state in the Labour government: Tony Benn, Michael Foot, and Peter Shore, together with the former Conservative minister Enoch Powell, noted for his strong views on the need to curb black immigration to Britain (see Benn, 1989, pp. 236–387). More recently, the coalition government established in May 2010 held a referendum in May 2011 to decide whether the country should stay with the "first past the post" system of voting—under which the candidate who secures the most votes in a constituency wins—or move over to an alternative vote (AV) system, where, if none of the candidates receives more than 50 percent of the votes, the process begins whereby, however long it takes, the one with the least number of votes is always eliminated and second preferences are distributed among the rest—until, eventually, one of the candidates emerges with a clear majority. While the Conservative Party was very much opposed to the AV system and their Liberal Democrat partners were strongly in favor, the Labour Party led by Ed Miliband was split on the issue, with former home secretaries David Blunkett and John Reid prepared to share a platform with David Cameron. It is on these occasions—others include the votes on capital punishment, environmental issues, human rights, the treatment of suspected terrorists, and decisions to go to war—when one realizes that the "line of demarcation" between parties can indeed be blurred and party loyalties can be fractured.

* * *

It will now be useful to examine briefly the historical origins of each of the three main political parties. It can be argued that only by understanding the nature of their development since the middle of the nineteenth century is it possible to appreciate the principles underpinning their evolving attitudes toward state education—and particularly at the secondary level.

* * *

The Conservative Party from Peel to the Present Day: From One-Nation Conservatism to New Right Neoliberalism

The Conservative Party is also often referred to as the Tory Party—the word "Tory" is believed to derive from the word "Toiridhe" or "Toraidhe," a term used to describe an Irish supporter of the House of Stuart to which the English monarchs belonged in the seventeenth century.

The ancestry of the modern Conservative Party has been variously traced; but it can probably trace its roots back to the emergence of a more clearly defined party system after the passing of the 1832 Reform Act, which began the long process of restructuring the electoral system in the United Kingdom. It is usually claimed that the word "Conservative" in its modern, strictly political sense was first used in an article in *The Quarterly Review* in January 1830: "We are now, as we have always been, decidedly and conscientiously attached to what is called the Tory, and which might with more propriety, be called the Conservative Party" (quoted in Blake, 1985, p. 6). Certainly, by the time Sir Robert Peel had become the acknowledged leader of the Conservative Party in 1835, the label "Conservative" had become one which could be usefully applied to all those ministers and politicians who wished to preserve the institutions of the state against radical innovation. It was, of course, a label that covered a wide range of political attitudes—from steadfast reaction to moderate reformism—but before a general election held in January 1835, Peel had taken the unprecedented step of issuing the Tamworth Manifesto of December 1834, which was an attempt to clarify the official policy of the party which he now led in the House of Commons. The publication of this document—recognized at the time as an important constitutional innovation—clearly afforded Peel the opportunity to inform his 586 constituents of the attitude of his government to some of the main political issues of the day. It opened by making it clear that Peel was making a plea to "that great and intelligent class of society...which is much less interested in the contentions of party than in the maintenance of good order and the cause of good government." Peel said he accepted the Reform Bill of 1832 as "a final and irrevocable settlement of a great constitutional question" and pledged himself and his colleagues to carry out "a careful review of all institutions, both civil and ecclesiastical," which would entail "the correction of proved abuses and the redress of real grievances." The Tory *Quarterly Review* was quick to recognize the constitutional significance of this set of electoral promises. An editorial published in April 1835 argued that: "in former times, such a proceeding would have been thought derogatory and impugned as unconstitutional, and would have been both; but the new circumstances in which the Reform Bill has placed the Crown, by making its choice of Ministers immediately and absolutely dependent on the choice of the several constituencies... have clearly rendered such a course of action not merely expedient but necessary" (*The Quarterly Review*, Vol. 53, April 1835, quoted in Briggs, 1959, p. 273).

In the 1985 edition of his book *The Conservative Party from Peel to Thatcher*, Conservative peer Robert Blake stressed the continuity of the

Party's social and political attitudes from the early nineteenth century to the mid-twentieth:

> The person who was a Conservative of the more thoughtful sort in Peel's day, his (sic) outlook, prejudices and passions, would have been quite recognizable to his counterpart who voted for Winston Churchill in the 1950s. There was a similar belief that Britain, especially England, was usually in the right. There was a similar faith in the value of diversity rather than uniformity, of independent institutions, of the rights of property; a similar distrust of centralizing officialdom, of the efficacy of government (except in the preservation of order and national defence), of Utopian panaceas and of "doctrinaire" intellectuals; a similar dislike of abstract ideas, high philosophical principles and sweeping generalizations. There was a similar readiness to accept cautious empirical piecemeal reform, but only if a Conservative government said it was needed. There was a similar reluctance to look far ahead or worry too much about the future; a similar scepticism about human nature; a similar belief in original sin, and in the limitations of political and social amelioration; a similar scepticism about the whole notion of "equality". (Blake, 1985, p. 359)

Professor Denis Lawton has pointed out that it can, in fact, be misleading to think of postwar Conservatism as essentially "ideology-free," with, at least until the 1970s, a dislike for "abstract ideas" and "sweeping generalizations." In his view, this often meant no more than "a preference for the status quo," which "can be just as much an ideological position as is a desire to change or reform institutions" (Lawton, 1994, p. 3). And even this fundamental characteristic of postwar Conservatism was to change when Margaret Thatcher assumed the leadership of the Conservative Party in February 1975 and set about transforming its image as the "common-sense" party, reluctant to embrace idealistic visions or radical solutions to social and economic problems.

Robert Blake has suggested that Benjamin Disraeli, who became the effective leader of the Conservative Party in the House of Commons in 1849, was in many ways the real founder of modern Conservatism, not only in the field of party organization, but also "in the far more important field of political ideas." In Blake's view, "it cannot be wholly accidental or erroneous that so many modern Conservatives look back on Disraeli as their prophet, high priest and philosopher rolled into one" (Blake, 1985, p. 3). But, once again, one has to bear in mind that Blake was writing at a time when the Conservative Party had not yet come to embrace many of the free-market values more usually associated with the nineteenth-century Manchester school of radical liberals led by industrialists like Richard Cobden and John Bright.

Disraeli believed in the necessity of gaining working-class support by stressing the identity of interests of different classes and groups in society and, where possible, ameliorating the obvious differences between them in wealth, income, and lifestyle. He had used his 1845 novel *Sybil* or *The Two Nations* to deplore the existence of "two nations" in Britain—the rich and the poor—"between whom there is no intercourse and no sympathy; who are as ignorant of each other's habits, thoughts and feelings, as if they were dwellers in different zones, or inhabitants of different planets; who are formed by a different breeding, are fed by different food, are ordered by different manners, and are not governed by the same laws" (*Sybil*, Book 2, Chapter 5), And Disraeli used a speech delivered at a Conservative banquet in Edinburgh in 1867 to return to his theme that the Conservative or Tory Party had to see itself as "the National Party of England":

> In a progressive country, change is constant; and the great question is not whether you should resist change which is inevitable, but whether that change should be carried out in deference to the manners, the customs, the laws and the traditions of a people; or whether it should be carried out in deference to various abstract principles and arbitrary and general doctrines. The one is a national system; the other...is a philosophic system.

He went on:

> Now I have always considered that the Tory Party is the National Party of England. It is not formed of a combination of oligarchs and philosophers who practise on the sectarian prejudices of a small portion of the people. It is formed of all classes, from the highest to the most homely; and it upholds a series of institutions that are in theory, and ought to be in practice, an embodiment of the national requirements and the security of the national rights.... Whenever the Tory Party degenerates into an oligarchy, it becomes unpopular; whenever the national institutions do not fulfil their original intention, the Tory Party becomes odious; but when the people are led by their natural leaders, and when,

by their united influence, the national institutions fulfil their original intention, the Tory Party is always triumphant, and then, under Providence, will secure the prosperity and the power of the country. (Quoted in Blake, 1966, p. 482)

After the Second World War, a significant body of opinion within the Conservative Party believed that it was time to revive Disraeli's "One-Nation" approach and to emphasize that society was not just a random collection of competing individuals. (As we shall see later in the chapter, this was a time when a large section of the political class in Britain was prepared to accept the basic assumptions of the newly created welfare state). Just before the Conservative Party conference in 1950, nine young Conservative MPs, with the official blessing of the party, published a book of essays covering a wide range of domestic policy issues. Having adopted the title of "One-Nation Conservatives" as their collective name, it seemed sensible to all those present at the planning meetings to call the book *One Nation: A Tory Approach to Social Problems*. And in his Foreword to the book, R. A. Butler, very much associated with the 1944 Education Act, picked up the theme that it was one of the Conservative Party's main tasks to promote the nation's sense of itself as a unity. The party, he insisted, had "a long and honourable record in the field of Social Service", which refuted the claim of the postwar Attlee government that "the Labour Party had a monopoly in this sphere." Admittedly, the Conservatives had lost successive general elections in 1945 and 1950; but their fortunes would revive, "provided they stayed true to Disraeli's message" (Butler, 1950, p. 7).

Writing in 1997, Ian Gilmour, a member of the One Nation Group of Conservatives from 1962 to 1992 and a minister in the cabinets of both Edward Heath and Margaret Thatcher, argued that a large section of the party was wrong to turn its back on the concept of "One-Nation" after Mrs. Thatcher defeated Edward Heath in the leadership election of February 1975. Although he accepted a post in the Foreign Office in the Thatcher government of 1979, he admits that "he never thought for a moment that the Thatcher Experiment would last," and when he was sacked in September 1981 he told the waiting reporters outside 10 Downing Street that "the Government was heading for the rocks." In his coauthored 1997 book *Whatever Happened to the Tories: The Conservative Party since 1945*, he reported that Mrs. Thatcher had once admitted to him that she did not really know what "One-Nation" meant, and that, on another occasion, she had made the astonishing claim that "One-Nation Conservatives" were really "No-Nation Conservatives" (Gilmour and Garnett, 1997, p. 1).

Margaret Thatcher came to power in May 1979 determined to change Britain. In her view, it had become an uncompetitive society in which the larger unions had too much power; too many adults were dependent on welfare benefits; and there were not enough people with a stake in the future of capitalism. Privatization and the breakup of state monopolies were to play a major role in her program to secure the regeneration of Britain, and the implementation of this program also necessitated a major change in the political philosophy of the Conservative Party. This was not, of course, a one-person crusade; and in her attempt to refashion the party as one with radical neoliberal ideas, Mrs. Thatcher had the support and encouragement of a number of enthusiastic devotees of the free market—notably Sir Keith Joseph and Alfred Sherman with whom she had founded the right-wing think tank the Centre for Policy Studies, in August 1974. Indeed, it has been argued by at least one influential commentator (see Young, 1989, pp. 87, 100) that Mrs. Thatcher did not enjoy a reputation as "an accomplished theoretician" in the early stages of her career, and that it was "entirely due to men like Joseph and Sherman" that the future leader came to "educate herself in liberal economics after 1974."

It is certainly true that Keith Joseph played a very significant role in the development of the new prime minister's political and social philosophy in the late 1970s. He had been at the Department of Health and Social Security (DHSS) in Edward Heath's 1970–1974 administration and might himself have stood for the leadership of the Conservative Party in February 1975 had he not been widely criticized for a controversial speech he delivered to the Birmingham Conservative Association in October 1974 in which he argued that the nation was moving toward inevitable degeneration on account of the high and rising proportion of children being born to mothers "least fitted to bring children into the world" (see Chitty, 2007, p. 100).

In a speech delivered to the Oxford Union in December 1975, Joseph argued that the Conservative Party was now "obsessed with the middle ground of politics." This was, in fact, "the lowest common denominator obtained from a calculus of assumed electoral expediency, defined not by reference to popular feeling, but by splitting the difference between

Labour's position and that of the Conservatives." The disastrous effect of this continuing adjustment by Conservative politicians in what they fondly believed to be the pursuit of votes could be described as "the Left-wing ratchet." Possessing no coherent philosophical position of their own, Conservatives felt obliged to make progressive and apparently unending concessions to a Left-dominated consensus. And this resulted in their adoption of policies favored by the Left, which, in turn, had the unhealthy effect of steadily extending the boundaries of the state (Joseph, 1976, p. 21).

It was now time to proclaim the supremacy of the market; in another speech, entitled "Moral and Material Benefits of the Market Order," delivered to the Bow Group of Conservatives in Norwich in July 1976, Joseph stated categorically that:

> The blind, unplanned, uncoordinated wisdom of the Market is overwhelmingly superior to the well-researched, rational, systematic, well-meaning, cooperative, science-based, forward-looking, statistically respectable plans of governments, bureaucracies and international organizations.

He went on:

> The market system is the greatest generator of national wealth known to Mankind: coordinating and fulfilling the diverse needs of countless individuals in a way which no human mind or minds could even comprehend, without coercion, without direction, without bureaucratic interference. (Joseph, 1976, pp. 57, 62)

The philosophy of the 1970s neoliberals, also often referred to as the New Right, can be seen as an expression of the new politics which emerged in both Britain and America in that decade in response to the major world economic recession that erupted in 1973–75, marking the decisive end of what was probably the longest and most rapid period of continuous expansion that world capitalism had ever enjoyed. While it would be wrong to see this recession as having a single cause, its onset was clearly marked by a quadrupling of oil prices by OPEC (Organization of Petroleum Exporting Countries) in 1973. It can be argued that it was indeed this economic recession of 1973–75 that fundamentally altered the map of British politics in the mid-1970s and provided the necessary conditions for the widespread dissemination of right-wing ideas. For Professor Andrew Gamble, writing in 1988, there were certain important beliefs which were common to all adherents of neoliberal or New Right philosophy:

> What all strands within the New Right share... is the rejection of many of the ideas, practices, and institutions which have been so characteristic of Social Democratic regimes in Europe and also of the New Deal and the Great Society Programmes in the United States. The New Right is radical because it seeks to undo much that has been constructed in the last sixty years. New Right thinkers question many of the assumptions which have become accepted for the conduct of public policy, while New Right politicians have sought to build electoral and policy coalitions which challenge key institutions and key policies.... These thinkers and politicians are all fierce critics of Keynesian policies of economic management and high public expenditure on welfare. But these New Right and neo-liberal politicians are also renowned as advocates of national discipline and strong defence.... To preserve a free society and a free economy, the authority of the state has to be restored. (Gamble, 1988, pp. 27–28)

There is, then, a paradox at the very heart of Thatcherite Far Right philosophy; and this is why, for Gamble, the phrase which best summarizes the doctrine of Keith Joseph and his associates (and the hegemonic project which it inspired) is: "Free Economy / Strong State."

It will be one of the aims of this book to trace the development of neoliberal ideas after Margaret Thatcher's downfall in November 1990 and to ascertain the extent to which they directly influenced New Labour education policy after 1994.

The Liberal Tradition since the Mid-Victorian Age: Liberals, Classical Liberals and Social Liberals

It is fair to say that the history of the Liberals / Liberal Democrats has been relatively neglected by academic historians and political commentators; there are a number of pretty obvious reasons why this has been so. More than a hundred years have passed since the great Liberal electoral landslide of January 1906, when Sir Henry Campbell-Bannerman's Liberal Party secured 377 seats in the House of Commons—and a majority of 84 over all other parties combined. The last Liberal prime minister, David Lloyd George, lost power in 1922; and the Liberal Party ceased to be a major force in British politics after the electoral debacle of October 1924, when the party gained a mere 40 seats. From now on, the Liberals were no longer able to harness a rising working-class political consciousness to their fading party; as the recently formed Labour Party grew in power and influence, the Liberal Party became, in the words of Chris Cook's *Short History of the Liberal Party*, "the Cinderella of British politics" (Cook, 2010, p. 1).

If there was a moment during the reign of Queen Victoria (1837–1901) when the Liberal Party can be said to have been born, it was probably on June 6, 1859 at a famous meeting in Willis's Rooms—a fairly substantial meeting place on St. James's Street in London—when a large group of leading Whigs, Peelites and radicals combined to get rid of the minority government of the Earl of Derby and Benjamin Disraeli.

It will be worth considering the characteristics and outlook of each of these groups in turn.

The Whigs had shared with the Tories (already featured in our section on the Conservative Party) the distinction of being the main political party in Britain in the eighteenth and early nineteenth centuries, the term "Whig" probably deriving from the word "Whiggamore," which was a contemptuous nickname given to the Scots Presbyterians of the seventeenth century. (Their attack on royalist forces in Edinburgh in the middle years of the seventeenth century was known as "the Whiggamore Raid"). Unlike the majority of Tories, the Whigs represented both the landed aristocracy and the moneyed middle class at the time of the Industrial Revolution. They spoke on behalf of industrialists, manufacturers, and religious dissenters for political and social change that would further their cause, but their reform program was extremely limited and successive Reform Acts in 1832 and 1867, which extended the franchise, also reduced their influence in the House of Commons. Within the Liberal Party, they constituted, in Chris Cook's phrase (Cook, 2010, p. 2), "an exclusive caste in the upper reaches of political society," and their dominant position in the House of Lords meant that they were able to hold high office in a number of Liberal administrations. From the 1850s onwards, they had to acknowledge the growing influence of the Peelites who owed much of their political philosophy—amounting to a more moderate and consensual form of

Toryism—to the reforming agenda of Sir Robert Peel who had died in a riding accident on Constitution Hill in 1850. It is, of course, interesting to note that William Gladstone should have seen himself as a Peelite on his journey from being a reactionary Tory and High Churchman to becoming leader of the Liberal Party in 1868—and, in the same year, prime minister for the first time. But, in the long term, it was the growing number of radicals, rather than the Peelites, who were to pose the more serious threat to the passivity and essential conservatism of the Whigs. These were, in a sense, the most "militant" and the most assertive of the individuals who made up the new Liberal Party; and the Group's most dynamic element was the nonconformist manufacturing interest. It was, in fact, from constituencies in Lancashire, Yorkshire, and the industrial Midlands that these radical dissenters and businessmen were chiefly returned. In their determination to challenge the existing order in both church and state and to put forward demands for the extension of the franchise and for the promotion of a form of state education, they were viewed with great suspicion by both the Whig hierarchy and the Whigs' allies among the large number of "moderate" Liberals, all of whom found the radicals' enthusiasm for change frankly disturbing.

From the very beginning, then, the Liberal Party was composed of many diverse elements, but it is important to stress that the balance of forces within the party, both at Westminster and in the country at large, did not remain static, and that, within a short space of time, differences within the party were to centre on differing conceptions of the nature of the state, foreshadowing the scene with which we are familiar today.

For many Liberals involved in politics in the closing decades of the nineteenth century, the radical program of unrestricted individualism was failing to take account of the needs of a rapidly changing industrial society. And these "Social Liberals" developed ideas on the merits of "collectivism" which were to exert a powerful influence on the policies of the pioneering Liberal administration elected in 1906.

Richard Grayson has argued that, for many Social Liberals, the key figure to be revered is the Liberal economist William Beveridge (1879–1963), whose famous report on *Social Insurance and Allied Services*, published at the height of the Second World War, identified five great giants that had to be slain on the "road to social reconstruction": want, disease, ignorance, squalor, and idleness. According to

Grayson, "there is a narrative popular with "Social Liberals," which runs along the lines of the Liberals under David Lloyd George establishing the welfare state after the election victory of 1906, with radical enhancements made following the Beveridge Report of 1942—a narrative that, while accepting that many important reforms were implemented by a Labour government, effectively makes Lloyd George and Beveridge "the true founders of the modern Welfare State" (Grayson, 2009, p. 53). This version of events clearly overlooks the extent to which the National Health Service was imagined only in outline by Beveridge, with detailed planning carried out by officials who had learned from the Emergency Medical Service—and the fact that it was actually implemented by the Labour Party after 1945, driven by Aneurin Bevan. And it also needs to be acknowledged that the declared aim of the Beveridge Report was not, in fact, security though a welfare state, but security by cooperation between the state and the individual.

It seems to be generally agreed that there are two dominant ideological traditions within the Liberal Democrats (the name of the party since the merger in March 1988 with the Social Democrats who had broken away from the Labour Party in March 1981): classical liberalism and social liberalism. A particular feature of an edited collection of essays published in 2009 (Hickson, 2009) is the emphasis placed on a third group within the modern Liberal Party: the so-called centrists, but, for our purposes, it will be sufficient to concentrate on the two distinct ideological perspectives that have underpinned mainstream Liberal thinking for over a century. And it is probably fair to say that it is the classical liberals, with their core belief in the effectiveness of the private sector, who have been in the ascendant in recent years, with the key text for understanding their philosophy, *The Orange Book: Reclaiming Liberalism*, published in 2004 (Marshall and Laws, 2004), provoking much discussion within the party on the nature of "freedom" and the precise role of the state in economic and social affairs. If there can be said to have been a clear social liberal response, it is probably *Reinventing the State*, published in 2007 (Brack, Grayson, and Howarth, 2007) arguing for a reinvention of the state along localized lines. The Coalition Agreement between the Liberal Democrats and David Cameron's Conservative Party after the May 2010 general election can possibly be viewed as some sort of "victory" for the classical liberals, and it is interesting to note that one of the chief negotiators at that critical time was David Laws, one of the editors of the 2004 *Orange Book*.

* * *

The Origins and Principles of the Labour Party: Marxist, Socialist, or Social Democratic?

Throughout the middle years of the nineteenth century, many people in Britain seemed to be enjoying some sort of "prosperity," although the country was clearly much divided and there was a huge and taken-for-granted gap between the lifestyle of the rich and that of the very poor. If this created a degree of complacency in the population, it was to be cruelly shattered by the social and economic trends of the century's final decades.

The 1870s triggered a long and heated debate about whether Britain was now entering a period of economic decline. After decades of undisputed industrial supremacy, the country was experiencing falling prices, narrower profit margins, and stiff competition from both German and American manufacturers who clearly benefited from larger domestic markets and greater natural resources. Looking back on this period in a speech made in Birmingham in May 1904, the leading late-Victorian politician Joseph Chamberlain argued that "the day of small nations has long passed away; the day of Empires has come" (quoted in Pugh, 2005, p. 11). Although Britain possessed an extensive and still-expanding empire, much of her overseas territory remained thinly populated and vulnerable to rival powers. Was Britain failing to exploit the economic potential of her imperial possessions? And beneath these growing concerns over industrial decline and the future of the Empire lay a fundamental unease about the moral and economic well-being of a large section of the working population.

The incomes of working-class families were particularly affected by the sharp rise in unemployment during the three serious slumps of 1879, 1886, and 1893–1894, a situation which had the effect of causing many workers to question the principles underpinning the existing social and economic framework. The mid-Victorian trade unions had campaigned for the right of skilled workers to negotiate a fair wage and to organize their own systems of insurance, but this left the forces of unskilled labor vulnerable to the unpredictable vagaries of free-market capitalism. The attraction of Socialist teaching, which was already an active political force on the Continent, lay in the fact that it seemed to provide a way forward out of the current economic malaise. If an unplanned capitalist economy must inevitably swing between "boom" and "slump," it was obviously necessary to devise new arrangements whereby the economy of the country might be planned and controlled. If the old unionists, and their allies within the Liberal Party, could not guarantee an assured standard of living for all workers, it was necessary for unskilled workers to demand a new political organization of their own. According to Socialist teaching, the slumps of 1879 and 1886 were not just isolated examples of bad luck or unfortunate circumstances, they were the clear manifestations of a corrupt and unworkable economic system that was inevitably doomed, and its demise must be hastened by effective working-class struggle.

It was after the second slump—the one that struck with devastating force in 1886—that a new stage in the movement to secure workers' rights was reached when a number of Socialist leaders began to organize large groups of unskilled workers, particularly in London. Open-air meetings in the capital were growing continually larger; and on one occasion, on November 13, 1887—known for many years as "Bloody Sunday"—a pitched battle took place in Trafalgar Square between the police and the crowd. In the end, the area had to be cleared by life guards, and, although the troops did not open fire, two of the demonstrators died from their injuries, and over a hundred became casualties. Then, two years later, in August 1889, the dockers of London, mostly classed as "unskilled workers," were organized by Ben Tillett, assisted by Tom Mann and John Burns of the Amalgamated Society of Engineers, in a demand for the so-called dockers' tanner: sixpence an hour, instead of fivepence an hour, or even less. The leaders of the dockers' strike succeeded in both maintaining peace and skillfully attracting nationwide sympathy, notably through a series of well-organized processions of strikers through the City of London. A total of £18,000 was raised in voluntary subscriptions, and another £30,000 was telegraphed by leading trade unions in Australia, so that fairly generous strike pay could be organized and other workers paid not to take the strikers' jobs. The propertied classes were, of course, much relieved when the "dockers' tanner," together with most of the dockers' other demands, were conceded by the employers after a month of action, in early September 1889.

In her 1992 biography of the great Socialist politician Keir Hardie, who was to become the effective leader of the Labour Party in parliament in 1906, Caroline Benn suggested that by the early 1890s, the Conservative and Liberal parties were probably congratulating themselves that "the parliamentary system was weathering labour unrest and making the transition to an increasingly enfranchised state relatively smoothly." But, as she also points out, "they were largely unaware of how quickly matters were moving where they could not see: in the working-class communities of Britain, and in certain radical middle-class groups" (Benn, 1992, p. 96). By 1892, the Scottish Labour Party already had 30 branches; in England, there were hundreds of independent Labour groups and Socialist societies, particularly in the north of the country. As these groups proliferated, interest rose in forming a national Labour Party; and at the 1892 Trades Union Congress, a motion calling for independent Labour representation was debated and carried.

Important events in the origins and early history of the Labour Party included: the founding of the Independent Labour Party in 1893, that of the Labour Representation Committee (LRC) in 1900, and the transformation in 1906 of the LRC into the Labour Party in parliament. It was recognized at the time that the truly sensational aspect of the general election of January 1906, which brought the Liberal Party under Sir Henry Campbell-Bannerman to power, lay in the fact that it brought the Labour Party 53 seats in the House of Commons. Of these, 29 were returned under the banner of the Labour Representation Committee; and of the remaining 24, a few were members of the Liberal-Labour group, but most were officials of the miners' union. An overwhelming parliamentary mandate gave the new Liberal government complete assurance in the House of Commons; but of far greater long-term significance was the fact that a growing political party now had effective representation in parliament.

Many historians have questioned whether the British Labour Party was ever truly socialist; it is certainly arguable that Marxist ideology in any meaningful sense was only one of many competing influences in the Labour Party's formative years. Nevertheless, it seemed essential to form an identity separate from that of the ailing Liberal Party; and, under the influence of such prominent left-wing thinkers as

G. D. H. Cole, who emphasized the need for effective worker control of industry, R. H. Tawney, who demanded greater social equality, and Harold Laski, who endorsed the idea of public ownership of major industries as a means of reducing class tensions, there were times in the first half of the twentieth century when the Labour Party appeared to be adopting a number of recognizably socialist objectives.

The famous (and now abandoned) Clause Four of the Labour Party's 1918 Constitution stated as its aim:

> To secure for the producers by hand and by brain the full fruits of their industry, and the most equitable distribution thereof that may be possible, upon the basis of the common ownership of the means of production and the best obtainable system of popular administration and control of each industry and service.

And Labour's election manifesto in 1945 listed a number of the key industries that would be nationalized in the event of a Labour victory at the polls—principally coal, iron and steel, the railways, long-distance road transport, civil aviation, gas and electricity, along with the Bank of England—as essential first steps toward the peaceful, democratic creation of a planned socialist economy. The Labour government's nationalization program was, in fact, successfully implemented between 1946 and 1949; in almost every case, something like a corporate model was introduced: that is to say, internal democratization was kept strictly limited (see Morgan, 1984, pp. 33, 98).

In the 50 or so years since the final electoral defeat of that great reforming postwar Labour administration in October 1951, many of its more radical measures have been reversed, notably as part of the privatization agenda of the 1979–1990 Thatcher government; and Labour has ceased to think of itself as, in any real sense, a socialist party.

Long before the election of Tony Blair as party leader in July 1994, there was an acceptance that the party's reforming zeal would never encompass major inroads into the power and influence of British capitalism. Indeed, the debate with right-wing opponents became centered on the best way of managing a capitalist economy and of securing conditions favorable to the accumulation of capital and to the assurance of ongoing profitability. And even the exact meaning of a watered down "social democratic" agenda was often left deliberately vague and open to varying interpretations. All of this meant that Labour supporters in the country were more impatient for radical change than could honestly be said of the majority of their representatives at Westminster.

In his 1963 Introduction to a new edition of Walter Bagehot's classic 1867 text *The English Constitution*, prominent Labour MP and diarist Richard Crossman made the somewhat cynical observation that, since the Labour Party could not afford to maintain a large army of paid party workers, it required the support of known "militants": "Politically conscious Socialists who would do the work of organizing the constituencies". Their commitment and enthusiasm were won through the propagation of two totally false propositions: that Labour was indeed a truly socialist party; and that sovereign powers lay in the hands of delegates at the Annual Party Conference (Crossman, 1963, pp. 41–42). The Marxist political philosopher Ralph Miliband (father of David and Ed) was thinking of both the Labour Party in Britain and the Democratic Party in the United States when he wrote in a book published in 1969 that:

> Social Democratic parties, or rather Social Democratic Leaders, have long ceased to suggest to anyone but their most credulous followers (and the more stupid among their opponents) that they were concerned in any sense whatever with the business of bringing about a Socialist society. (Miliband, 1969, p. 273)

And, more recently, in a discussion with Doreen Massey for the political journal *Soundings*, leading sociologist Stuart Hall has talked of the Labour Party, or New Labour, becoming "disconnected from its political roots" and evolving into the "second party of capital" (Hall and Massey, 2010, p. 59).

A reluctance to acknowledge the need for radical social change has had a marked effect on the Labour Party's attitude towards education since the Second World War—as we shall see in later chapters.

From Keynesian Social Democracy to a Post–welfare Society

With these brief accounts of the historical origins of the main political parties serving as the context for our discussion, it will now be useful to concentrate on the period since the Second World War and examine the extent to which these parties either differed or agreed on major issues of social policy, including education. Specifically, in which decades, and for what reasons, was either consensus or conflict the dominant feature of the political debate?

As we have seen, both Socialist and Liberal politicians and their advisers were anxious to claim the credit for many of the principles underpinning the postwar welfare state, but it is also true that many Conservative politicians of the period—and particularly those belonging to the "One-Nation" tradition within the party—accepted the need for a degree of significant social change. Indeed, the word "Butskellism" came to be used to describe a political program cutting across traditional party lines—the word being made up of the name of the Conservative politician R. A. Butler (already cited in an earlier section) and that of Hugh Gaitskell, who succeeded Clement Attlee as leader of the Labour Party in 1955.

In the view of leading political commentator Professor David Marquand, a Labour member of parliament from 1966 to 1977 and later a prominent member of the breakaway Social Democratic Party, it was in the postwar period—an elastic term, lasting in this case for as long as 30 years—that Britain's political class shared a tacit governing philosophy that might be called "Keynesian Social Democracy." This philosophy did not cover the whole spectrum of political opinion, nor did it prevent vigorous party conflict. The Conservative and Labour Parties often differed fiercely about specific details of policy, and, at a deeper level, their conceptions of political authority and of social justice differed even more. But they differed within a structure of generally accepted values and common assumptions. And, in David Marquand's view, it was this structure that was of overwhelming significance:

> For most of the post-war period, most front-benchers in the House of Commons, most senior civil servants, most of the leaders of the most powerful trade unions, most nationalized industry chairmen (sic), most heads of large private-sector companies and most commentators in the quality press shared a common experience and a broadly similar set of aspirations. They were determined to banish the hardships of the pre-war years, and to make sure that the conflicts which those hardships had caused did not return. Thus, both front benches accepted a three-fold commitment to full employment, to the Welfare State and to the co-existence of large public and private sectors in the economy—in short, to the settlement which had brought the inter-war conflicts to an end. (Marquand, 1988, p. 3).

Within this "postwar settlement," there was a special place for the 1944 Education Act, which came to be regarded by many as a cornerstone of the welfare state. The act sought to establish secondary education for all pupils as an integral part of a new view of education, to be seen henceforth as a continuous process—ranging from the primary sector to further education. And this would be achieved within the administrative framework of "a national system, locally administered." Being a source of much pride at the time, this system involved the continuing operation of a benign partnership between central government, local government, and individual schools and colleges.

The 1950 report of the Ministry of Education (which was actually published in 1951) was intended to celebrate the 50-year history of a unified central department established as a consequence of the 1899 Board of Education Act; it began with a joint introduction by George Tomlinson (minister of education from 1947 to 1951) and his permanent secretary Sir John Maud, which emphasized that the postwar system was actually building on a structure which had already made a significant contribution to the democratic life of the nation:

> This is the story of a progressive partnership between the central department, the local education authorities and the teachers. To build a single, but not uniform, system out of many diverse elements; to widen educational opportunity and, at the same time, to raise standards; to knit the educational system more closely into the life of an increasingly democratic and industrialized community: these are among the main ideas which, despite two major wars, have moved legislators and administrators alike. (Ministry of Education, 1951, p. 1)

This "single, but not uniform system," with its clear emphasis on the importance of "partnership," was seen in 1945 as a peculiarly British response to the dangers inherent in the centralizing tendencies which had been so obvious in other parts of Europe. The tripartite partnership that existed between central government, local government, and the individual schools and colleges seemed to contemporaries to involve a network of checks and balances that ensured the effective diffusion of power within the education system and thereby prevented the imposition of what might be seen as undesirable policies.

It seems clear that the postwar Keynesian social democratic consensus survived many strains and stresses in the 1950s and 1960s. Where education was concerned, there were major disagreements between the two major parties, at both national and local level, as to the merits or otherwise of the new comprehensive or multilateral schools established to take children of all "abilities" at the age of 11, but this did not involve a questioning of the role and status of local education authorities. Indeed, their standing appeared to be enhanced when the Labour government's 1965 circular (Circular 10/65), by which comprehensive secondary education became national policy, requested rather than required local authorities to prepare plans in their areas for comprehensive reorganization.

The postwar Keynesian consensus, or what Labour politician Tony Benn labeled as "the welfare capitalist consensus" (Benn, 1987, p. 301) could claim many achievements. Although it was a seriously flawed formation, which relied on dynamic and ceaseless capitalist growth to create the wealth for redistribution, its full-employment philosophy, welfare support schemes and plans for universal health care and for the expansion of higher education, transformed the lives of millions of people in the postwar years. As we have already seen, it finally collapsed in the mid-1970s, as a deep economic recession fundamentally changed the map of British politics. It simply could not survive a combination of mounting inflation, swelling balance of payments deficits, unprecedented currency depreciation, rising unemployment, bitter industrial conflicts, and what seemed to many observers to be ebbing governability.

The breakdown of the consensus meant that the 20-year period after 1976—the year when Labour chancellor Denis Healey had to appeal for help from the IMF (International Monetary Fund)—was to be one of genuine political conflict between the two main parties at Westminster. This was the period when the Conservative leadership began to embrace a new updated version of the classical market liberalism of the nineteenth century. As far as education was concerned, it was no longer clear that a Conservative government was actually committed to the administrative framework for state education that had existed since 1944.

It was Margaret Thatcher's third education secretary, Kenneth Baker (May 1986 to July 1989), who was called upon to pilot through parliament the most far-reaching piece of education legislation since the passing of the 1944 Act. And its radical nature can hardly be exaggerated; for the central purpose of the 1988 Education Reform Act (ERA) was that power should be gathered to the centre and, at the same time, devolved on to schools and parents, both processes being at the expense of mediating bureaucracies, whether elected or not. Writing in *The Independent* on June 11, 1987, the day of the 1987 general election, education journalist Peter Wilby had forecast: "The election of a Conservative government today will mean the break-up of the state education system that has existed since 1944."

The main centralizing feature of the 1988 act was the introduction of a new national curriculum for all state primary and secondary schools in England and Wales. The creation of a new tier of schooling designed, at least in part, to undermine the power and influence of local education authorities, involved the introduction of City Technology Colleges (CTCs) and Grant-Maintained (or GM) Schools. The new CTCs for 11- to 18-year-olds—around 20 in number and to be situated largely in inner-city areas—would be financed partly by the private sector and would be completely independent of local authority control. GM schools would be those schools, both secondary and large primaries, where a requisite proportion of parents voted to take the school out of local control and the school would then receive direct funding from the central government.

As Peter Wilby had correctly anticipated, what all this meant in practice was the abandonment of the essential principles that had governed the organization of schools since 1944. A national system in the hands of quite powerful local education authorities was to be replaced by a network of separate, semiautonomous institutions, maintained either by local authorities or by the Department of Education and Science. Since another feature of the 1988 act was that, henceforth, the delegated budget to schools would be determined by a formula largely reflecting the number of pupils on the school roll, it was clear that the local authorities' analysis of need was to be replaced by market concepts of demand, and that resources were to be distributed according to the new principle of consumer choice. The notion of a publicly planned and provided education service had been effectively challenged so that state education should ultimately become a commodity to be purchased and consumed.

It will be one of the arguments in the chapters that follow that a period of genuine political conflict, when the Labour front bench challenged the Conservatives' education policy on a number of fronts, came to an end in the mid-1990s, after the untimely death of John Smith on May 12, 1994 and his replacement as Labour Party leader by Tony Blair.

It soon became clear that the new leader and his shadow education spokesperson, David Blunkett, were anxious to jettison many of the Labour Party's traditional commitments on education—particularly with regard to the future of 11-plus selection. There was indeed to be a new period of consensus, but this time it was to be a consensus largely on the Right's terms and one that rejected most of the guiding principles of the "welfare capitalist consensus" of the postwar years.

Surveying the educational scene in Britain from 1945 to 2005 in the second edition of her book *Education in a Post–welfare Society*, first published in 2001, Professor Sally Tomlinson, an adviser to the Labour Party in the early 1990s, argued that this was a period during which "government in the UK moved from creating and sustaining a welfare state, to promoting a post–welfare society, dominated by private enterprise and competitive markets." In this new "post–welfare society," there had, she argued, been "a fragmentation of social welfare programmes," largely as a result of the introduction of market principles, and, by 2005, education, subject to these same market principles, had clearly become "a competitive enterprise and a commodity, rather than a preparation for life in a modern democratic society" (Tomlinson, 2005, p. 1). Since this is a widely held view of the changing nature of official attitudes toward the role and function of education, it will be one of the principal aims of this book to ascertain to what extent such attitudes have been sustained and promoted under a series of New Labour governments from 1997 to 2010.

Chapter 3

Labour Education Policy, 1944–1994: 50 Years of Missed Opportunities and Uneasy Compromises

The Origins of the Common Schooling Debate

Any study of the fate of secondary education under New Labour will inevitably have to focus on the debate on how schools should be organized for children once they have reached the age of 11. Indeed, this debate has been the source of a remarkable degree of friction within the modern Labour Party.

The fight for a common secondary or "comprehensive" school has its roots deep in the Labour Movement, dating from at least the first half of the nineteenth century, when the working class in Britain was struggling to establish itself as an independent political force. The idea that education should be provided in a series of common schools organized in ascending stages was put forward by leaders of the London Working Men's Association, precursors of the Chartists, as long ago as 1837 (see Simon, 1960, p. 258).

It was not, however, until the end of the century, and the formation of many new radical political movements, that common education for all ages was advocated widely in Britain. At an international conference of Socialists held in London at the Queen's Hall in Langham Place in July 1896, delegates from all over Europe and the United States pressed for a full education for all working people. At this event, Britain's Keir

Hardie spelled out what form it had to take: free at all stages and open to everyone, without any tests of prior attainment at any age—in effect, a comprehensive "broad highway" that all could travel, regardless of their circumstances (reported in *The Westminster Gazette*, August 1, 1896, and quoted in Benn, 1992, p. 135). But the emerging Labour Movement was not united on this issue, and opposition came in particular from the distinctly moderate Fabian Society, which took a more elitist position on educational matters. One of its leaders, Sydney Webb, favored the idea of specialized and differentiated schooling at the secondary stage, together with a "capacity-catching" scholarship system acting as a sort of "educational ladder," by means of which the "clever" working-class child could rise out of its impoverished circumstances. Webb strongly backed the fee-paying grammar schools provided for in the 1902 Education Act which offered a limited number of free scholarship places. According to Webb, writing in 1908, the duty of the nineteenth century in education was merely to supply

> enough schools for all the children, and then to get the children into them. The twentieth century recognizes that its task is the more complicated one of providing every part of the country with the highly differentiated educational organization necessary to ensure to every child the particular kind of schooling that it needs. (Webb, 1908, p. 289)

Webb noted with satisfaction that the provision of generous scholarships and free places meant that even the children of the poor could gain access to "first grade" secondary schools: those in which "a fair proportion of the pupils, however young may be their age at entrance, may be expected to remain until the age of eighteen or nineteen" (p. 292). He went on to observe that the social distinction between elementary and secondary education had everywhere been "blurred" and sometimes even "practically obliterated" since the great bulk of the population could, by means of free places and scholarships, by entrance examinations and judicious selection, have access to "just the kind and grade of schooling that their attainments and idiosyncrasies required" (p. 29).

Despite strong working-class opposition to the development of different types of secondary schools, the principle of differentiation was clearly well-established by the time R. H. Tawney's all-important *Secondary Education for All: A Policy for Labour* was published in 1922.

This report, prepared by a respected Socialist and economic historian, for the Education Advisory Committee of the Labour Party, became in effect the basis of the party's education program in the interwar years. Tawney believed that the very assumption on which the education system was based, that something called "elementary education" was all that the child of the workers could benefit from—"as though the mass of the people, like anthropoid apes, had fewer convolutions in their brains than did the rich"—was in itself "a piece of insolence" (Tawney, 1922, p. 33). He looked forward to a situation where, instead of only a minority of children from the elementary school gaining entry to a secondary school by means of a free place or scholarship, "all normal children, irrespective of the income, class or occupation of their parents," would be entitled to receive a free secondary education. But these secondary schools would, of course, be "various in type"; and "not all children would pass to the same kind of school." Although all youngsters would spend the critical years from 11 to 16 under "the invigorating influence of a progressive course of full-time education," it would not be practicable for a single common school to cater to the needs of all adolescents" (pp. 7, 78). To this extent, the philosophy underpinning Tawney's report was in line with the thinking of the leading educational psychologists who acted as advisers to the governments of the day.

As Michael Parkinson argued in a book published in 1970, confusion in Labour thinking as to the exact meaning of Tawney's "secondary education for all" continued throughout the interwar years—and into the period when the Labour Party formed the government of the country after 1945 (see Parkinson, 1970, p. 48). Since for many Labour Party supporters, the whole idea of a secondary education was associated with a grammar-school education, it seemed quite inconceivable that the party should contemplate "sacrificing" the grammar school in favor of a different and untried type of secondary system. In other words, the grammar school had implicitly become the party's model for the development of secondary education, and this was so despite the selective nature of its entry. At the same time, the grammar school was seen as playing an important practical role as the main avenue of occupational and social mobility for working-class children, and this was another reason for its popularity. It is, of course, important to note at this point that the party's emotional attachment to grammar schools served to sidestep the all-important question as to what proportion of children could actually benefit from a strictly academic secondary education. As we shall see later, the Labour government's 1965 circular "The Organization of Secondary Education" found it convenient to promote the new "comprehensive" schools as "schools which will preserve all that is really valuable in a grammar-school education for those children who now receive it, and make it available to more children" (DES, 1965, p. 1). This was Hugh Gaitskell's concept of comprehensive schools as being, in effect, "grammar schools for all."

The 1944 Education Act and Its Aftermath

As we saw in chapter 2, the 1944 Education Act sought to extend educational opportunity by providing free secondary education for all as part of a new system, to be seen as a continuous process ranging from the primary school to further or higher education. The school-leaving age was to be raised to 15 (though this was not, in fact, implemented until 1947), and provision was made for a further rise to 16 "as soon as the Minister is satisfied that it has become practicable,"—this eventually took place in 1972/73. In 1938, the last full year before the outbreak of the Second World War, nearly 40 percent of children above the age of 11 were still being taught in the senior classes of all-age elementary schools. Now all children were to receive a proper secondary education, although, in the event, the act contributed very little to the debate on how that secondary education should be organized. There seemed to be an assumption that secondary schooling should be provided in different types of schools; but comprehensive or multilateral schools were not officially proscribed. Section 8 of the act stipulated that:

> the secondary schools available for an area shall not be deemed to be "sufficient," unless they are sufficient in number, character, and equipment to afford for all pupils opportunities for education offering such variety of instruction and training as may be desirable in view of their different ages, abilities, and aptitudes, and of the different periods for which they may be expected to remain at school. (Education Act, 1944, p. 5)

But this section of the act was open to a number of different interpretations; and the ambiguity in the wording meant that when the pressure for reform of the system became almost irresistible in the 1960s, it could be carried out by simply reinterpreting the formula, without the need for further legislation. Indeed, attention was drawn to the possibility of experimenting with new multilateral schools, even while the bill was under discussion in parliament, by an experienced educational administrator, J. Chuter Ede, the Labour parliamentary secretary to the Board of Education. "I do not know where people get this idea about three types of school," he said in a speech delivered in April 1944, "because I have gone through the Bill with a small toothcomb, and I can find only one school for senior pupils—and that is a secondary school. What you like to make of it will depend on the way you serve the precise needs of the individual area in the country" (*The Times*, April 14, 1944, quoted in Rubinstein and Simon, 1973. p. 31). Despite a reputation for strong radical sympathies, reinforced by the publication in 1939 by the Left Book Club of her moving study of Jarrow, the town in north-east England deeply affected by the Depression of the 1930s (*The Town That Was Murdered*), Ellen Wilkinson, the first Labour minister of education (1945–1947) in the postwar Attlee administration, was not prepared to challenge existing orthodoxy where the organization of secondary schools was concerned. She certainly made little attempt to undermine the prevailing philosophy of her ministry that embraced a firm commitment to a tripartite system of secondary education—grammar, technical and modern schools—and a deep mistrust of multilateral and comprehensive schools. The new minister was herself a successful working-class product of the divided state education system, having won a scholarship at the age of 11 to Ardwick Higher Elementary Grade School in Manchester; and it has been suggested by historian Brian Simon that this probably colored her outlook (Simon, 1974, p. 284). According to a study of the 1945–1951 Labour government published in 1984: "Ellen Wilkinson embodied Labour's instinctive faith in the grammar schools, the bright working-class child's alternative to Eton and Winchester" (Morgan, 1984, p. 174). Whatever the motivation, she made her position perfectly clear, soon after taking up her post, at a meeting in London. It was not, she declared, her intention "to destroy the grammar schools." They were, she went on, "the pioneers of secondary education and... it would be folly to injure them.... The most urgent need in the field of new developments was an adequate number of modern secondary schools, because more than half the children of secondary age would attend these schools" (*Education*, October 2, 1945, quoted in Fenwick, 1976, p. 54).

Although Ellen Wilkinson was not prepared to respond to pressure from the National Union of Teachers and from the National Association of Labour Teachers to sanction multilateral or comprehensive experiments on a large scale, it is the view of her biographer Betty Vernon that she was sometimes less dogmatic on the issue than is commonly acknowledged "I want to make it clear," the minister told the House of Commons in July 1946, "that there is no antagonism in my mind to the actual idea of multilateral or bilateral schools... but I do want to see that the proposals are properly worked out and that the schools do not become unreasonably large" (*Hansard*, H. of C., Vol. 424, cols. 1811–12, July 1, 1946, quoted in Vernon, 1982, p. 217). At the same time, it has to be pointed out that she did not accept the argument, common on the Left, that the tripartite system was educationally and socially divisive. In her view, the provision of one-third of a pint of milk free to all pupils under the age of 18—an innovation welcomed in those days of austerity—should be seen as "the culmination of our (the Labour Party's) promise to do away with class distinction." Speaking at the 1946 Labour Party Conference, she went on to point out: "Free milk will be provided in Horton and Shoreditch, in Eton and Harrow. What more social equality can you have than that?" (Quoted in Vernon, 1982, p. 214).

Ellen Wilkinson's successor in office, George Tomlinson (1947–1951), accepted wholeheartedly the divided nature of the British educational system, not even wanting to get rid of the public schools. Indeed, he went out of his way, in a 1947 debate on education in the House of Commons to emphasize that "it is no part of our policy to reduce in any way the status or standing of the grammar school" (quoted in Fenwick, 1976, p. 57). And, on receiving a hostile memo in 1950 from a committee set up by the National Executive Council of the party to review its policy towards secondary schooling, the minister declared that "the Labour Party are kidding themselves if they think that the comprehensive idea has any popular appeal" (quoted in Parkinson, 1970, p. 47). According to his biographer Fred Blackburn, Tomlinson had a very limited vision of his role as minister, even though he had always desperately wanted the job, so that during his period in office, the general lines of government policy were invariably determined by ministry officials and civil servants (Blackburn, 1954, p. 6). Apart from a rigid devotion to the new tripartite system, he is now chiefly remembered for a remark that "minister knows now't about curriculum" (see Lawton, 1980, p. 31). When the Labour government fell in 1951, *The*

Times Educational Supplement of October 19 wrote, approvingly, that "it was extremely doubtful whether Mr. Tomlinson ever once lifted a hand to increase the number of the country's comprehensive schools" (quoted in Rubinstein and Simon, 1973, p. 39).

Throughout the 1950s, while the Labour Party was in opposition, there was little indication that the party was capable of adopting a united stance on the issue of secondary reorganization.

A report prepared by the committee appointed earlier by the NEC, and published in June 1951 as *A Policy for Secondary Education*, questioned the validity of the secondary tripartite system, and especially the fairness of 11-plus selection, and also attempted to draw up a blueprint for a successful comprehensive school; but the endorsement of a new type of secondary system was somewhat cautious and half-hearted (see Fenwick, 1976, p. 63). Later policy statements such as *Challenge to Britain* in 1953 and *Learning to Live* in 1958 embraced more positive proposals for the reorganization of secondary education along comprehensive lines; but there was still ambiguity in Labour thinking as to the likely fate of grammar schools. It was not clear that the party at large was yet in a position to contemplate their demise. In one of his diary entries for October 1953, Labour MP Richard Crossman noted how Labour Party conference delegates were "relatively conservative on all educational matters" and retained a deep emotional and intellectual attachment to the grammar schools. He observed that "nearly all the delegates either were at grammar school or have their children at grammar school, and are not quite so susceptible to the romantic Socialism of the 1920s and 1930s" (see Morgan, J., 1981, p. 270). This was certainly true of the delegates from Wales where Labour had swept the board in the 1945 election and which was very much a stronghold of the grammar schools. It was recalled that Lloyd George had once described Pengam Grammar School as "the Eton of Wales" (quoted in Morgan, K., 1981, p. 106).

Admiration for what grammar schools had to offer was particularly strong among the working classes, and the late writer and broadcaster Edward Blishen has written of how he was made well aware of this while teaching in a tough secondary modern school in a neglected, deprived part of north London from 1949 until the late 1950s:

> Secondary education for all has a fine ring about it; but is it yet more than an aspiration? And what does "secondary education" actually mean?

> In the districts with which I am familiar, the people, justly enough, take it to mean a grammar-school education. ("I mean, this isn't a real secondary school," said a parent to me once, stubbornly incognisant of the signboard at the school entrance.) And they don't precisely mean grammar-school education in its every detail. They have in mind the fact that grammar schools take their pupils somewhere, strengthen them, and add to them, palpably and measurably. The grammar school has managed to become something much more than a place to which you have, by law, to send your child for a specified period. It's a road that forks out in many directions, not one that comes to a single dead end. (Blishen, 1957, p. 75)

And these perceptive comments were later confirmed by William Taylor in his 1963 study of the secondary modern school:

> It is clear that, for the working-class child, the grammar school not only provides education that makes upward social and occupational mobility practicable, but also furnishes an educational and social environment which encourages the formulation of upwardly mobile vocational aspirations. (Taylor, 1963, p. 80)

Politicians might talk about "parity of esteem" and the need to provide different types of secondary schools for different types of pupils, but nothing could alter the simple fact that in the view of many, if not the majority of parents, both middle-class and working-class, only the grammar school was capable of providing a genuine form of secondary education.

At a time when the Labour Party was debating issues raised in the document *Learning to Live*, opposition to the party's (albeit tentative) support for the comprehensive principle and concern about the implied threat to the future of the grammar schools, were expressed with some vigor by veteran Labour MP Emanuel (Manny) Shinwell in a letter he wrote to *The Times* at the end of June 1958:

> We are afraid to tackle the public schools to which wealthy people send their sons (sic), but, at the same time, we are ready to throw overboard the grammar schools, which are, for many working-class boys, the stepping-stones to universities and a useful career. I would rather abandon Eton, Winchester, Harrow and all the rest of them than sacrifice the advantage of the grammar school. (Letter to *The Times*, June 26, 1958)

And this letter provoked an interesting response a week or so later from Labour leader Hugh Gaitskell who, in his own letter to *The Times* at the beginning of July, rejected Shinwell's accusation that grammar schools were being "thrown overboard," and put forward the far more positive (if hardly realistic) suggestion that comprehensive schools were a means of ensuring that the benefits of a grammar-school education would be spread far more widely:

> It would be nearer the truth to describe our proposals (in *Learning to Live* and elsewhere) as "a grammar-school education for all."... Our aim is greatly to widen the opportunities to receive what is now called "a grammar-school education," and we also want to see grammar-school standards, in the sense of higher quality education, extended far more generally. (Letter to *The Times*, July 5, 1958)

This policy statement can be seen as a neat way of reconciling two conflicting points of view: on the one hand the comprehensive reform would obviously mean the demise of the grammar schools as separate institutions; at the same time, all the essential elements of what they had to offer would be retained in a different form.

Gaitskell's view of Labour Party education policy was reiterated several times by Harold Wilson (Gaitskell's successor as party leader from 1963 onwards) in the period leading up to the 1964 general election. Despite the embarrassment caused to many educationists and teachers—and particularly those party members who had, for a decade or more, supported the idea of genuine comprehensive schools for educational and egalitarian reasons and had strong views about the limited value of the grammar school model—the new slogan of "grammar schools for all" in fact served a number of useful functions. It silenced the opponents of comprehensive reorganization within the party itself; it appealed to growing demands for a more meritocratic system of secondary education; and it dispelled the fears of parents who had placed their trust in the traditional grammar-school curriculum. Writing in 1982, sociologist David Hargreaves expressed his admiration for the slogan, but pointed out that there came a time when people found it less than convincing:

> The slogan was indeed a sophisticated one, for it capitalized on the contradictions in the public's mind: parents were in favour of the retention

of the grammar schools and their public examinations, but opposed to the 11-plus selection test as the basis of a "once-for-all" allocation. If the comprehensive schools could be seen by the public as "grammar schools for all," then the contradictions could be solved. And many people seem to have accepted this argument, at least for a short period, and at least in principle. But it can be argued that public opinion is notoriously fickle; and when comprehensive reorganization actually began and many grammar schools had to be closed, as part of their amalgamation into the new comprehensive schools, immediately a strenuous defence of the grammar schools was activated. (Hargreaves, 1982, p. 66)

Whatever their views as to the merits or otherwise of the 11-plus selection process, very few parents campaigned for the retention of the secondary modern schools. Indeed, the new schools were dismissed as failures almost as soon as they were born—a common criticism in the postwar period being that they were merely the old elementary schools writ large. In his acclaimed first novel *Roaring Boys: A Schoolmaster's Agony*, published in 1955 and based largely on his experiences as a young English teacher at Archway County Secondary School for Boys in north London, Edward Blishen painted a vivid picture of the sort of world he was entering when he began teaching in a tough urban secondary modern school—here called "Stonehill Street"—at the end of the 1940s:

> Every morning, the school would come into view, as unkind as a prison. It wasn't of the worst period of State school architecture: it was only two storeys high, instead of three; there were warm red bricks distributed among the grey ones; and a curve here and there in the roof-line had a sort of mollifying effect. But the architect was definitely thinking of prisons when he designed it. Its gates were so obviously meant to be locked; its high walls were so plainly meant to imprison; its hard playgrounds were so suggestive, not of play, but of penal exercise. And over the doors were worn announcements in stone: "Senior Boys," "Senior Girls." These words were no longer relevant, but their terse statement of categories made it easy to imagine the mute pinafored ranks of fifty years before. (Blishen, 1955, p. 16)

And this view of the physical environment in which many secondary modern school teachers were expected to work was reiterated by Gary McCulloch in a study that was published in 1998:

> In many cases, the buildings in which the secondary modern schools were housed and the neighbourhoods that they served gave them the reputation of "slum schools." The accommodation of the schools in the form of their buildings and facilities often reflected their pre-history as elementary, senior and central schools that had catered principally for working-class children, to such an extent indeed that they struggled to justify their new status as "secondary schools." (McCulloch, 1998, p. 80)

From the very beginning, secondary modern schools faced a very real problem in that, unlike the grammar and public schools, they lacked, and indeed were never given, a clear sense of their aims and objectives. Should they opt for a diluted version of the traditional subject-based grammar-school curriculum, particularly for those pupils in the higher streams; or should they plan something that was completely different, with little or no regard to the demands created by entering young people for external examinations? For those pupils who bitterly resented failing the 11-plus examination, the curriculum on offer in many modern schools seemed both impoverished and undemanding. University teachers Paul Dash and Chris Searle are among those who have written of the humiliation and sense of rejection felt by all those aspiring youngsters forced to attend a poorly resourced secondary modern school where nothing was expected of them—in the case of Paul Dash, a two-form entry school on the Cowley Road in Oxford, and in the case of Chris Searle, a small secondary modern school in London. These writers talk of the lack of laboratories and equipment for anything but the most rudimentary science; of libraries that consisted of little more than a few shelves in a cupboard; and of a total absence of facilities for gymnastics or games (see Dash, 2002; 2012; Searle, 2001). At the other end of the spectrum, there was the story of a secondary modern school for girls serving a poor working-class district in a large industrial city, which took in only those pupils who had failed to get into either a grammar or a selective central school, and where the 23 girls entered for the GCE (General Certificate of Education) examination in 1954 achieved a total of 78 passes (Simon, 1955, p. 66). And it was this type of story that helped to make the case for the view that it was impossible to tell, from the results of tests administered at the age of 11, what a child's future accomplishments might be.

From Circular 10/65 to the Ruskin Speech

By the time the Conservatives were defeated in the 1964 general election and the Labour Party was back in power with a very slim majority of just four seats, there was widespread popular disenchantment with the divided system of secondary schools that had been in existence for the past 20 years. And it was clear that in the years leading up to this electoral defeat, a social movement of considerable significance was taking place in the country. In 1960, the number of pupils being educated in comprehensive schools in Britain amounted to less than 5 percent of the secondary school population, and then, in the four years between 1960 and 1964, roughly a quarter of all local education authorities were making major changes in their selection procedures. It really did seem as if what author C. P. Snow attacked (in the final section of his famous 1959 lecture *The Two Cultures*) as "the rigid and crystallized pattern" of English education was beginning to break up under the weight of its inherent contradictions. Indeed, looking back on this defining moment in postwar educational history, in an article published in 1972, Edward Boyle revealed with characteristic candor that on becoming Conservative education minister in July 1962, it was obvious to him that "support for the development of Secondary Education along comprehensive lines was gaining considerable momentum" (Boyle, 1972, p. 32). It was for this reason that advocates of reform were able to argue that the Labour government's decision to make comprehensive schooling a national policy, far from being "radical" or "revolutionary" in character, was simply a matter of responding to, or taking account of, local initiatives of a widespread nature. In the words of Dr. Keith Fenwick:

> With the advent of a Labour government in 1964, national and local policies came largely into line; and Circular 10/65 seemed an acceptable progression of policy to many in education who were not themselves ardent supporters of comprehensive reorganization. (Fenwick, 1976, p. 158)

It was only when the general commitment to change became specific to individual and often prestigious secondary schools that a clear focus for local opposition was provided, which, in turn, helped to fuel the national Conservative backlash of the second half of the 1960s.

Anthony Crosland, the talented politician who became education secretary in January 1965, was already known to be a fervent supporter of comprehensive education. In *The Future of Socialism* published in 1956 and *The Conservative Enemy* published in 1962, he had written that class had replaced capitalism as the principal dragon to be slain and that educational reform of a far-reaching nature was the most effective means of creating an efficient classless society. In the words of his friend and admirer Roy Hattersley, his great strength—"tragically, almost unique in the Labour Party after the defeat of the Attlee Government in 1951"—was his "absolute and total confidence in the superiority of egalitarian socialism over all other philosophies" (Hattersley, 1997, p. 180). And, according to his wife and biographer Susan Crosland, he cared so passionately about the cause of secondary reorganization that, on one occasion in the Spring of 1965, following a difficult day battling with his officials at the DES (Department for Education and Science) followed by dinner with four of the teachers' associations, he informed her angrily that "if it's the last thing I do, I'm going to destroy every f......g grammar school in England. And Wales. And Northern Ireland" (Crosland, 1982, p. 148). This was somewhat at odds with Harold Wilson's famous claim that grammar schools would be abolished "only over his dead body."

When Crosland arrived at the DES at the beginning of 1965, there was already a draft comprehensive school circular in existence that had been drawn up by his immediate predecessor Michael Stewart. From two conversations that Crosland had later, in the Autumn of 1970, with Maurice Kogan, professor of government and social administration at Brunel University, we learn that the early months of 1965 were dominated by a lively debate within the department as to whether the new circular (later known as Circular 10/65) should require or simply request the 163 local education authorities in England and Wales to prepare plans for comprehensive reorganization in their areas. We know that Crosland finally sided with those of his officials opting for "request"; and he told Kogan in 1971 that in coming to this decision, he had been strongly influenced both by his meetings with the Association of Education Committees and by his judgment of "the general mood of the local authority world" (Kogan, 1971, p. 189). While those working at the DES were still divided on the issue, he made it very clear in a House of Commons debate held toward the end of March 1965 that he was anxious to avoid compulsion. "I am perfectly confident," he said, "that local authorities will respond voluntarily and co-operatively to our request to submit reorganization plans" (reported in *The Times Educational Supplement*, March 26, 1965). And asked by Kogan if he regretted not taking statutory powers back in 1965, Crosland was most emphatic in his response:

> No. You must remember that, at that time, most local authorities were Labour-controlled and sympathetic to what we were doing—as indeed were some Tory authorities. So the plans were coming in at least as fast as we could cope with them. For the whole time I was at Curzon Street (the DES), the thing was going as fast as it could possible go. In fact, the limitation was one of human and physical resources, and not one of statutory powers. But, of course, the situation changed later when the disastrous local election results of 1968 and 1969 put the Tories into power almost everywhere. (Kogan, 1971, p. 191)

Crosland was always very anxious in 1965 to play down any suggestions in the national press of bitter conflict between his department and a number of recalcitrant LEAs, by reminding everyone, in the meetings that he addressed, that almost two-thirds of the secondary school population already lived in areas where the local authority was either implementing or planning a comprehensive schools policy. As he pointed out in a speech delivered at the end of May, it was not a case of the Labour government imposing comprehensive education on a reluctant nation:

> The fact is that there has been a growing movement against the 11-plus examination and all that it implies. And this movement has not been politically inspired or imposed from the Centre. It has been a spontaneous growth at the grass-roots of education, leading to a widespread conviction that separation is an offence against the child, as well as a brake on social and economic progress.... The whole notion of a selection test at this age belongs to the era when secondary education was a privilege of the few, and this is generally understood. (Quoted in Kerckhoff et al., 1996, p. 28)

Crosland also recognized that the LEAs possessed unique local knowledge, and seems, therefore, to have respected the fact that there was undoubtedly more expertise to oversee reorganization in the various localities than existed within his own overstretched ministry.

The circular that the department published on July 14, 1965 began by announcing that it was the government's declared objective "to end selection at 11-plus and to eliminate separatism in secondary education." Local education authorities were requested to submit, within a year, "plans for reorganizing secondary education in their areas on comprehensive lines." No single pattern of comprehensive organization was specified. Instead, the circular outlined the "six main forms" of organization that had "so far emerged from experience and discussion." Four of these would be regarded as "fully comprehensive," while two would be acceptable only as "interim solutions," and "the simplest and best solution" (provided the local authority could devise a viable scheme without having to take account of existing buildings) was the "all-through" 11–18 comprehensive school already established in parts of London, Coventry, and elsewhere.

The four patterns recognized as "fully comprehensive" were:

1. The orthodox comprehensive school for pupils aged 11–18;
2. A two-tier system, whereby all pupils transferred automatically at 13 or 14, without any form of selection, to a senior comprehensive or upper school;
3. A two-tier system, comprising schools for the 11–16 age range, combined with new sixth form colleges for those over the age of 16;
4. A two-tier system, comprising new "middle schools" for pupils aged 8–12 or 9–13, followed by "upper schools" with an age range of 12 or 13 to 18.

The two patterns regarded as "acceptable" for only a transitional period involved the use of separate schools for pupils over the age of 13 or 14 and the continuance of some form of selection. In one of these, older pupils had to choose between a senior school catering for those who expected to stay at school well beyond the compulsory leaving age and a senior school catering for those who did not.

It was accepted that "the most appropriate system" would depend on "local circumstances," and that an authority might well decide to adopt "more than one form of organization" in a single area. It was also made clear that the government did not seek to impose "destructive or precipitate change on existing schools"; and it was recognized that "the evolution of separate schools into a comprehensive system" must be "a constructive process requiring careful planning by the local education authorities in consultation with all those concerned" (DES, 1965, pp. 1, 2, 10, 11).

Whatever might be said in favor of the consensual approach that Crosland adopted in 1965, many of the serious problems facing comprehensive schooling in England and Wales in the late 1960s and 1970s could, in fact, be attributed to the cautious and tentative nature of Circular 10/65. Characterized in *The Guardian* (July 14, 1965) as "an amiably toothless tiger" and as "a vague and permissive document" in *The Times Educational Supplement* (December 31, 1965), it tried hard to avoid causing offence, without settling many of the major problems that were associated with comprehensive reorganization. It stated categorically that no extra money would be made available to assist the process of change before at least 1967–68 (ibid., p. 11), which effectively meant that many of the new comprehensive schools had to begin life in buildings designed for use as separate establishments. Then again, the range of patterns that would be considered "acceptable" as comprehensive schemes—even if only on a temporary basis—was so great as to create the widespread suspicion that the resulting system would resemble "a patchwork quilt" of uneven quality. In particular, the decision to sanction the use of parallel schools for pupils over the age of 13 or 14 and the continuance of some form of selection seemed to be a denial of everything that comprehensive education was supposed to stand for. Research carried out by John Eggleston for the journal *New Society* into the working of the two-tier Leicestershire Plan, which had been launched in 1957 and where only those pupils who gave an undertaking that they would sit external examinations could transfer from the middle or high school to the upper school at the age of 14, clearly indicated that in this case *academic* selection had been replaced by a form of *social* selection. Put simply, it was predominantly middle-class parents who chose an extended education for their older children (Eggleston, 1965). And above all, the decision to avoid going down the road of compulsion in 1965 was of questionable validity. It might have worked if the spirit of "consensus" had been genuinely "national"; but between 1965 and 1970, a number of local authorities, mainly but not exclusively Conservative-controlled, were able to make eye-catching headlines in the national press by boasting of decisions that clearly flouted the spirit and intentions of the circular. Many of the leading campaigners for comprehensive education would have welcomed the drafting of a solid and cogently worded piece of legislation—particularly after the March 1966 general election, which gave Harold Wilson's Labour Party a healthy House of Commons majority over all other parties of 97, with the heady prospect of a full five-year term in government.

The wording of Circular 10/65 was symptomatic of the confusion that existed, both within the government and within the Labour Party at large, as to what comprehensive schooling actually amounted to in practice—beyond the abolition of the 11-plus and the amalgamation, where appropriate, of existing grammar and secondary modern schools. Some of these conflicting ideals and aspirations have been referred to earlier in the chapter; but it is worth pausing at this stage in the narrative to gauge their significance and relevance.

For leading comprehensive school campaigners such as Caroline Benn and Brian Simon, the comprehensive reform was largely about promoting the idea of human educability and challenging the fallacy of fixed potential in education. The 11-plus selection examination was inherently flawed because it was based on the theory that the level of "intelligence" or "intellectual ability" that any child could reach was already determined by biological mechanisms. And it could be argued that the whole postwar education system was based to a recognizable extent on determinist theories of human intelligence put forward by the leading psychometrists of the day, and notably by Cyril Burt and Hans Eysenck. Burt himself recognized the implications of his theories when he argued in a BBC radio Third Programme talk broadcast in November 1950 that:

> Obviously, in an ideal community, our aim should be to discover what ration of intelligence nature has given to each individual child at birth, then to provide him (sic) with the appropriate education, and finally to guide him into the career for which he seems to have been marked out. (Reprinted in *The Listener*, November 16, 1950)

It was of considerable help to Benn and Simon's campaign that the very first Chapter of the 1963 Newsom Report, *Half Our Future*, a report concerned with the education of 13- to 16-year-old youngsters of "average or less than average ability," contained the famous unequivocal statements: "Intellectual talent is not a fixed quantity with which we have to work, but a variable that can be modified by social policy and educational approaches.... The results of recent investigations increasingly indicate that the kind of intelligence which is measured by the tests so far applied is largely an acquired characteristic. This is not to deny the existence of a genetic endowment; but, whereas that 'endowment,' so far, has proved quite impossible to isolate, a number of social and environmental factors can be identified" (Ministry of Education, 1963, p. 6). And in his Foreword to this 1963 report, the Conservative education minister Edward Boyle implicitly rejected the arguments of the psychometrists by stating that the essential point we have to grasp is that "all children should have an equal opportunity of acquiring intelligence, and of developing their talents and abilities to the full" (p. iv).

For Benn and Simon, and many other leading campaigners of the 1950s and 1960s, it made little or no sense that the new comprehensive schools should be promoted by some politicians as "grammar schools for all." Apart from any other considerations, this "flawed" concept meant that insufficient attention was paid to the creation of a whole-school curriculum, appropriate for institutions catering for a wide range of abilities and talents. And yet this formula was repeated in the first paragraph of Circular 10/65, where reference was made to the endorsement of government education policy by the House of Commons in a motion passed on January 21, 1965:

> That this House, conscious of the need to raise educational standards at all levels, and regretting that the realization of this objective is impeded by the separation of children into different types of secondary schools, notes with approval the efforts of local authorities to reorganize secondary education on comprehensive lines, which will preserve all that is valuable in a grammar-school education for those children who now receive it and make it available to more children (DES, 1965, p. 1; *Hansard*, H. of C., Vol. 705, col. 541, January 21, 1965)

As we have already noted, the slogan of "grammar schools for all" was to yield diminishing returns as the 1960s progressed. As well as being obliged to perpetuate all the elitist assumptions of a grammar-school education, at least for the pupils in their "top" streams and sets, the new comprehensive schools of the 1960s also suffered from being burdened with a bewildering array of unrealistic expectations.

As we saw in our earlier account of the views of Anthony Crosland, it was possible to argue that the comprehensive reform could be a crucial tool in the worthy process of improving British society, without recourse to violent or revolutionary change. In other words, the new comprehensive schools would constitute a step on the road to achieving greater equality—in the sense that working-class children would now be able to move into "white- collar" occupations or proceed to higher education. The leading sociologist A. H. Halsey could begin a widely quoted article "Education and Equality" in the journal *New Society* in June 1965 with the ringing declaration:

> Some people, and I am one, want to use education as an instrument in pursuit of an egalitarian society. We tend to favour comprehensive schools, to be against public schools, and to support the expansion of higher education. (Halsey, 1965, p. 13)

Yet, on closer examination, it seems clear that Crosland was mainly anxious to ally himself with "reformist" and Fabian elements within the Labour Party, which saw the comprehensive reform as having the strictly more limited social objective of creating a more cohesive and harmonious society. One of the central arguments of *The Future of Socialism*, published in 1956, was that comprehensive schools would enable children coming from widely different social backgrounds to meet and respect one another—thereby playing a leading role in the task of combating class hatred. According to Crosland:

> The object of having comprehensive schools is...to avoid the extreme social division caused by physical segregation into schools of widely divergent status and the extreme social resentment caused by failure to win a grammar-school place, when this is thought to be the only avenue to a "middle-class" occupation. (Crosland, 1956, p. 272)

This concept of the "social mix," while conveniently ignoring all the basic realities of British capitalist society, gained a tremendous hold on the Labour Party's imagination in the 1960s. With its keen anticipation of the steady amelioration of social class differences through pupils' experience of "social mixing" in a common secondary school, it possessed obvious appeal for all those who were looking for a palatable form of "social engineering" that did not involve any degree of social disruption.

The concept found expression in Circular 10/65 where an attempt was made to define what a genuine comprehensive school should aim to achieve:

> A comprehensive school aims to establish a school community in which pupils over the whole ability range and with differing interests and backgrounds can be encouraged to mix with each other, gaining stimulus from the contacts and learning tolerance and understanding in the process. But particular comprehensive schools will reflect the characteristics of the neighbourhood in which they are situated; if their community is less varied, and fewer of the pupils come from homes which encourage educational interests, schools may lack the stimulus and vitality which the schools in other areas enjoy. The Secretary of State therefore urges local authorities to ensure, when determining catchment areas, that the new schools are as socially and intellectually comprehensive as is practicable. (DES, 1965, p. 8)

One of the definitions of a comprehensive school, used as a basis for the research project sponsored by the DES and initiated by the National Foundation for Educational Research (NFER) in 1966, was that of a secondary school that "collects pupils representing a cross-section of society in one school, so that good academic and social standards, an integrated school society, and a gradual contribution to an integrated community beyond the school may be developed out of this amalgam of varying abilities and social environments" (Monks, 1968, p. xi).

This preoccupation with social objectives and the pursuit of an ill-defined "classlessness" was heavily criticized by Caroline Benn and Brian Simon in *Half Way There*, their 1970 report on the British comprehensive school reform. Here they argued that it was naïve to expect that comprehensive schools could, by themselves, bring about a more egalitarian society or that "the mere act of reorganization" would solve all social tensions. In their words: "A comprehensive school is not a social experiment; it is an educational reform" (Benn and Simon, 1970, p. 64).

This preoccupation with social unity, however defined, also had the unintended effect of setting up convenient targets for the diehard opponents of comprehensive schooling to aim at. It was possible to argue, as did R. R. Pedley, headteacher of St. Dunstan's College in southeast London, writing in 1969 in *Fight for Education*, the first of five black papers attacking the progressive education agenda of the Left, that supporters of the comprehensive project were using schools "directly as tools to achieve *social* and *political* objectives." It was easy for him to ridicule that "Utopia of Equality," where "the Duke lies down with the docker and the Marquis and the milkman are as one." Indeed, it was Pedley's view that class divisions were actually perpetuated and strengthened inside the comprehensive school: "4A doesn't mix with 4P, and the Cabinet Minister's son (or daughter) shows no particular eagerness to bring the bus conductor's child home to tea" (Pedley, 1969, p. 47). When Julienne Ford's researches in the late 1960s (Ford, 1969) led her to the conclusion that the comprehensive schools did not necessarily break down class barriers, this was immediately seen as proof that the comprehensive reform was a failure.

This confusion as to the real aims and objectives of comprehensive schooling meant that in the ten years following the promulgation of Circular 10/65, the supporters of the comprehensive reform were not exactly united in articulating precisely what they were fighting for. This disunity played into the hands of the opponents of reform at a time when the optimism of the 1960s was giving way to the disillusionment of the 1970s. We have already seen in chapter 2 that by the middle of the 1970s, the postwar consensus was beginning to break down on a number of fronts. And nowhere was this disintegration more apparent than in the case of education. The comprehensive system had, in fact, come under attack from a number of different directions since the final years of the 1964–1970 Wilson administration, and there had been a significant political dimension in that, within the Conservative Party, there had been a determined and ultimately successful campaign to reject Edward Boyle's largely "non-partisan" or even "bi-partisan" approach to education reform.

By the time Edward Boyle finally relinquished his post as shadow education minister in 1969, it was clear that he had lost the support of a large number of local party activists for his policy of "welcoming" experiments in comprehensive schooling. For some time, he had been aware of the exposed nature of his position on the "liberal" wing of the party—a position that became increasingly untenable as large groups of right-wing backbenchers and constituency workers mobilized against him (see Knight, 1990, pp. 22–60). Matters had come to a head at the 1968 Conservative Party conference, where Boyle was challenged to acknowledge that the party was hopelessly divided on such important issues as comprehensive reform and the future of the grammar schools, and where he made a passionate plea for moderation and consensus:

> I will join with you willingly and wholeheartedly in the fight against Socialist dogmatism wherever it rears its head. But do not ask me to oppose it with an equal and opposite Conservatism dogmatism, because in education, it is dogmatism itself which is wrong. (Quoted in Corbett, 1969, p. 785)

The plea was unsuccessful, and Boyle's official motion on education rejecting a confrontationist approach was defeated.

A key role in mobilizing opposition to Labour's reform agenda was played by the five black papers published between 1969 and 1977 (Cox and Dyson, 1969a and 1969b; Cox and Dyson, 1970; Cox and Boyson, 1975; Cox and Boyson, 1977). Indeed, Stephen Ball has viewed the publication, in March 1969, of the first black paper, *Fight for Education*, as marking neatly and symbolically "the beginning of the end of the period of optimism" (Ball, 1984, p. 4). It has been largely overlooked by commentators on the period, that there were, in fact, significant differences between, on the one hand, the three black papers published in 1969 and 1970 and, on the other, those published in 1975 and 1977. In the late 1960s, the Right in Britain was still seen as being on the defensive, fighting a rearguard action against an educational consensus of which it heartily disapproved. The early black papers could be viewed as a response to the widespread student unrest of 1968 and contained a number of spirited attacks on the associated concepts of comprehensive education, egalitarianism and "progressive" teaching methods. The various contributors were united in wanting to put back the clock: to the days of formal teaching methods and streaming in primary schools, of high academic standards associated with a grammar-school education, and of well-motivated, hard-working and essentially conservative university students. It was only in the last two black papers that support was given to the introduction, at least on a trial basis, of education vouchers and to the idea of providing much greater scope for parental choice of secondary school. As I have argued elsewhere (Chitty, 1989a, p. 52), it was in the eight years from 1969 to 1977 that the thinking of the Old Right gave way to the New—that "the politics of *reaction* gave way to the politics of *reconstruction*."

The Labour Party was thrown on the defensive by the ferocity and scale of the right-wing attacks on its education policies. The leadership appeared to be particularly embarrassed by the association of the party in the eyes of the public with so-called progressive education—characterized as it often was by a child-centered approach to teaching, informal pedagogic and assessment methods, and by a general antipathy to all manifestations of hierarchy and inequality. The controversy surrounding events at William Tyndale Junior School in Islington in north London between 1973 and 1975 served to provide a central focus in the backlash against "progressive" teaching methods, and occupied several column inches in the London and national press. When the Auld report on the school was published in 1976 (Auld, 1976), it seemed to indicate what could happen when a group of "unaccountable" and "politically motivated" individuals with radical educational views were allowed to take over the day-to-day running of a school.

In the light of contemporary trends, there appeared to be some justification for the triumphalist tone adopted by prominent right-wing Conservative MP and former comprehensive school headteacher Rhodes Boyson, when he addressed a meeting organized by NCES (National Council for Educational Standards) in May 1976 and boasted that "the forces of the Right in education are on the offensive. The blood is flowing from the other side now" (reported in *The Times Educational Supplement*, May 21, 1976).

The speech that Prime Minister James Callaghan delivered at Ruskin College, Oxford, on October 18, 1976 can be seen, in part at least, as an attempt to wrest the populist mantle from Margaret Thatcher's Conservative Party, and to pander to perceived public disquiet at the alleged decline in educational standards in state schools (see Chitty, 1989a, p. 95). The early black papers, and large sections of the popular press, had played a major role in undermining public confidence in the comprehensive system; and popular reservations about "progressive" or informal teaching styles appeared to be justified by the William Tyndale case and by stories about indiscipline and poor classroom management in comprehensive schools. One daily newspaper (*The Daily Mail*) had even gone so far as to "plant" a journalist-cum-teacher in a large south London comprehensive school, with the obvious intention from the outset of unearthing material damaging to the reputation of that school in particular and of comprehensive schools in general. The resulting articles, which appeared in the paper in March 1972 under such flamboyant headlines as "The Comprehensive Jungle" and "Chaos in the Comprehensives," were attacked by both staff and pupils for misrepresenting the facts and producing a distorted impression of day-to-day life at the school (see Chitty, 1979, p. 157). In the Ruskin speech, Callaghan referred to the new "informal methods of teaching," which might produce excellent results when they are in well-qualified hands, but are "much more dubious when they are not." At the same time, the speech was designed to highlight the need to make more effective use of the money—roughly £6 billion a year—that the government was spending on the nation's schools. The means of achieving this involved the construction of a new educational consensus around more central control of the school curriculum, greater teacher accountability and more direct subordination of the secondary-school curriculum to the "needs" of the economy.

Reacting to the Conservatives' Agenda

In the period from 1979 to 1997, Labour could do very little but react to the "radical" education policies being pursued by education ministers in the Thatcher and Major administrations. As we saw in chapter 2, the Conservatives' right-wing education agenda included an emphasis on providing more choice and diversity within the secondary system and on creating a more hierarchical system of secondary schools, subject both to market forces and to much greater control by the central government. New types of secondary schools would reintroduce (or simply reinforce) the principle of selection and would serve to undermine the power and influence of local education authorities. Although the move was effectively blocked by DES civil servants, Margaret Thatcher's second education secretary Sir Keith Joseph (1981–1986) even flirted with the idea of introducing the education voucher, whereby all parents would be issued a free basic coupon, fixed at the average cost of schools in the local authority area, to be cashed in at the school of their choice. The whole idea was, in fact, dropped when it was made clear to Sir Keith that the scheme he favored was financially and politically impracticable (see Chitty, 1997b, p. 82).

This was also the period when the Conservatives were seriously anxious to promote the idea of private sponsorship of schools. The original concept of the City Technology Colleges (CTCs), as announced by Education Secretary Kenneth Baker at the 1986 Conservative Party conference, was that private sector sponsors would be encouraged to contribute to the heavy capital costs of setting up the new colleges and that these new CTCs, situated largely, though not exclusively, in deprived inner-city areas, would be completely independent of local education authority control. And this was a time when the Labour Party was opposed to any example of creeping privatization in education, so that when it was becoming clear by the Autumn of 1988 that very few sites could be found for the new schools and that, in many areas, attempts to increase their number were foundering for lack of commercial support, Jack Straw, who was Labour's education spokesperson from 1987 to 1992, was happy to describe Kenneth Baker's CTC program as "An educational and political disaster" (quoted in *The Independent*, September 15, 1988).

Surveying the period from 1979 to 1990, Professor Sally Tomlinson has concluded that, despite a number of setbacks, "Thatcher's Government offered a coherent ideological approach to education centered on notions of a free economy and deregulated markets, promising choice, competition and excellence, along with a clear respect for tradition and hierarchy. Those on the Left were slow to realize all the implications of this, and were taken aback at the speed with which the Thatcher Governments set about changing the direction of the whole education system" (Tomlinson, 2005, p. 27). It can be argued that Labour's problem was that it could not be seen to be against choice and diversity, but, at the same time, it was well aware of the basic inequalities that Conservative policy produced. Until 1994, it was Labour policy to attack the underfunding of state education, while promising the early return of grant-maintained schools and CTCs to the local authority fold. In the case of 11-plus selection and the future of the remaining grammar schools, there was still a degree of confusion as to where the Labour Party stood; we shall return to this in the next chapter.

It was Labour's fourth successive electoral defeat, in the 1992 general election that caused a major reappraisal of education policy, including the decision to take over major elements of the Conservatives' education program.

Chapter 4

A Change of Direction: The Origins of New Labour's Education Philosophy

The Conservative Legacy

The radical ideas that had underpinned the 1988 Education Reform Act were also promoted by the education ministers who served Margaret Thatcher's successor as prime minister, John Major, in his two administrations, between 1990 and 1997.

Yet, although there was no lack of reforming zeal, there was a sense of disappointment that changes to the education system, particularly at the secondary level, were not happening with the sort of speed anticipated. The original 1986 City Technology College (CTC) brochure had, for example, given details of 27 locations where the new CTCs could be built (DES, 1986, p. 15), but difficulties with finding a sufficient number of wealthy sponsors, and suitable and inexpensive sites in the sort of areas envisaged in the initial plans, meant that when the CTC at Kingswood in Bristol opened in September 1993, it was, in fact, the last such college to be authorized, bringing the final total to just 15.

Then, according to a comprehensive analysis carried out by Local Schools Information (LSI) and published in February 1992 (LSI, 1992), schools wanting to opt out of local authority control and become new grant-maintained schools were concentrated in only 12 of the 117 education authorities in England and Wales. These 12 authorities (Bromley, Dorset, Ealing, Essex, Gloucestershire, Hertfordshire, Hillingdon, Kent, Lincolnshire, Norfolk, Northamptonshire, and

Surrey) accounted for 219 (or just over 50 percent) of the 428 decisive opt-out ballots. At the same time, a hugely disproportionate number of opt-out ballots had been held in selective grammar schools: a total of 57, thereby affecting 37 percent of the grammar schools then in existence. Of the 428 ballots held, voters in 97 schools had been opposed to opting out, with 331 in favor.

It was the task of Education Secretary John Patten, who acquired the portfolio in April 1992, to experiment with new ways of reintroducing forms of secondary selection at 11—without returning to the days of the discredited tripartite secondary system. And one of the new ideas was to be "selection by specialization." In an article that Patten wrote for the *New Statesman and Society*, published on July 17, 1992 under the title "Who's afraid of the 'S' word?" the education secretary argued that it was time for Socialists to come to terms with the all-important concept of specialization at the secondary level. In his words:

> Selection is not, and should not be, a great issue for the 1990s, as it was in the 1960s. The S-word for all Socialists to come to terms with is, rather, "Specialization." The fact is that children excel at different things; it is foolish to ignore it, and some schools may wish specifically to cater for these differences. Specialization, underpinned by the National Curriculum, will be the answer for some—though not all—children, driven by aptitude and interest, as much as by ability.
>
> It is now clear that on to the foundation-stone of the National Curriculum can be built the liberation of all the talents through greater specialization in all our secondary schools. This could be specialization within a large comprehensive school, setting for this or that subject—by the pupils self-selecting, or being guided towards their choice by aptitude and commitment. Or it could be something that builds on to the schools: a leading edge in bilingually taught technology, for example, or in music, or in the area where languages crucially meet business studies.
>
> Such schools are already emerging. They will, as much more than mere exotic educational boutiques, increasingly populate the new educational landscape of Britain at the end of this century—a century that introduced universal education at its outset; then tried to grade children as if they were vegetables; then tried to treat them...like identical vegetables; and which, while doing so, never ever gave them the equality of intellectual nourishment that is now being offered by the National Curriculum, encouraged by testing and audited by regular inspection. (Patten, 1992, pp. 20–21)

John Patten's white paper *Choice and Diversity: A New Framework for Schools*, published on July 28, 1992, claimed that since the Conservative election victory in 1979, five great themes had characterized educational change in England and Wales: quality, diversity, increasing parental choice, greater autonomy for schools, and greater accountability (DfE, 1992, p. 2). It went on to vilify the comprehensive system of secondary schools for "presupposing that children are all basically the same and that all local communities have essentially the same educational needs." And it asserted that "the provision of education, and particularly secondary education, should be geared more to local circumstances and individual needs: hence the Government's commitment to diversity in education" (pp. 3–4).

At the same time, the authors of the white paper were at pains to emphasize that *specialization* should never be confused with *selection*:

> The fact that a secondary school is strong in a particular field may well increase the demand to attend; but it does not necessarily follow that selective entry criteria have to be imposed by the school. The selection that does take place is always parent-driven. The principle of open access remains. As the demand to attend increases, it is, of course, true that the school may require extra resources to cope with the range of talent available. (p. 10)

The government wanted to ensure that there would always be "parity of esteem" between different schools, and the National Curriculum was there to help ensure "equality of opportunity" (ibid).

The principle of providing a greater variety of schools, particularly at the secondary level, was extended further, in a 1996 white paper *Self-Government for Schools*, published during Gillian Shephard's period as education secretary (1994–1997). The general tone of the document was set in an early section bearing the title "Choice, Diversity and Specialization," where it was argued:

> Children have different abilities, aptitudes, interests and needs. These cannot all be fully met by a single type of school—at least at secondary level. The Government wants parents to be able to choose from a range of good schools of different types, matching what they want for their child with what a school offers. The choice should include schools which select by academic ability, so that the most able children have the chance to achieve the best of which they are

capable.... Independent schools, church schools and grammar schools have long offered choice for some parents. The Government has greatly expanded diversity through the Assisted Places Scheme, by setting up the 15 City Technology Colleges, and by giving all secondary schools the opportunity to become grant-maintained. It has also encouraged schools to specialize in particular subjects, such as Technology and Modern Languages. (DfEE, 1996, pp. 2–3)

By the time this white paper was published in June 1996, there were still 163 grammar schools in England and Wales, concentrated in English counties such as Buckinghamshire, Kent, and Lincolnshire and in many of the larger conurbations; there were about 1,100 grant-maintained schools, including 660 secondary schools, accounting for almost one in five of all pupils at the secondary level; and there were 196 specialist schools and colleges: 15 CTCs, 30 language colleges and 151 new technology colleges. If the 1996 white paper had become law, grant-maintained schools would have been free to select up to 50 percent of their intake by general ability, or by ability or aptitude in particular subjects, without any need for central approval; language and technology colleges up to 30 percent; and all remaining LEA schools, where appropriate, up to 20 percent. As it happened, Conservative plans for an even more divided secondary system had to be jettisoned as a result of Tony Blair's victory in the 1997 general election.

What Was the Blair Project?

The death of Labour Party leader John Smith on May 12, 1994 was followed by a contest for the leadership of the party involving three senior party figures: Margaret Beckett, Tony Blair, and John Prescott. With Tony Blair's former close ally Gordon Brown having been "persuaded" to stand down, the leadership election results, declared on July 21, produced few surprises. Blair achieved 57 percent of the total vote, doing best with MPs (and MEPs), 65 percent of whom gave him their vote, and also securing the backing of 58 percent of party members and 52 percent of trade unionists (see Seldon, 2004, p. 198). In his acceptance speech on the day itself, Blair made the bold claim: "We can change the course of history and build a new, confident land of opportunity in a new and changing world" (quoted in Rentoul, 2001, p. 246).

The new leader had reached the conclusion, shared by many of those with whom he chose to work, that the Labour Party had to change both its policies and its image if it wanted to avoid a fifth successive electoral defeat. Blair did not, in fact, believe that John Smith could have won the next election pursuing the sort of traditional Labour policies he had been advocating since 1992. In the Introduction to his political memoir, *A Journey*, published in 2010, he conceded that his own politics "consciously and deliberately reached beyond traditional Left or Right" (Blair, 2010, p. xvii). And he went on to maintain that, although he had never held political office, "not even as the most junior of junior ministers," he had a clear strategy for guiding the Labour Party "from Opposition into Government," which involved redefining the party as "A changed progressive force in British politics" (p. 1). Yet what exactly was this "new progressive force" and how far did it intend to deviate from the concept of "democratic socialism" associated with previous Labour administrations?

A front-page article in *The Guardian* dated August 5, 2000, reported that the scholars working on *The New Penguin English Dictionary* had taken an unprecedented two months to arrive at a meaningful definition of the term "Blairism." Apparently, the first 16 words of the definition posed very few difficulties: "Blairism, *noun*: the policies associated with Tony Blair, British Labour Leader and Prime Minister from 1997"; but almost every word and phrase suggested for the rest of the sentence proved to be controversial and problematic. Early drafts included: "Especially regarded as a highly modified or modernized form of traditional Socialist thinking intended to appeal to a wider electorate"; "Characterized by the absence of a fundamental underlying ideology and by a close attention to prevailing public opinion"; and "Characterized by a modified and inclusive form of traditional Socialism." But all were rejected on the grounds that they were thought likely to cause offence. The final version of the second half of the sentence, consisting of just nine words that seemed to command widespread acceptance, had the essential virtues of being both bland and unexceptional: "Especially regarded as a modified form of traditional Socialism." The compilers of this section of the dictionary were well aware that Blair and his allies had deliberately set out to be vague (or, rather, all-encompassing) about their overall philosophy in order to make a real success of what has been called big-tent politics.

In a speech delivered on June 18, 1994 to a Fabian Society / *Guardian* conference under the title "Whatever Next?" (and reprinted later as a Fabian Society pamphlet), Tony Blair set out to explain, albeit in fairly general terms, what he meant by the term "Socialism." He argued that the Socialism of Marx, of centralized state control of industry and production, was dead. In Blair's view, this outdated form of Socialism "misunderstood the nature and development of a modern market economy; it failed to recognize that the state and public sector can become a vested interest, capable of oppression quite as much as the vested interests of wealth and capital; and it was based on a false view of class that became too rigid to explain or illuminate the real nature of class division today" (Blair, 1994, p. 3). In its place, Blair proposed a set of values or beliefs—loosely defined as "Ethical Socialism"—based around the notion of a strong and active society committed to promoting the needs of the individual and of enlightened self-interest. The basis of this new form of Socialism, or, to use Blair's preferred spelling, "Social-ism," lay in the view that individuals were "socially interdependent human beings" and that "the collective power of all should be used for the individual good of each." If Socialism could be defined in this way, rather than as the promotion of a set of "narrow timebound class or sectional interests" or as a collection of "particular out-of-date economic prescriptions," then it could liberate itself, "learning from its history, rather than being chained to it" (p. 4). Blair claimed that if and when he became prime minister, he did not want to run "A Tory economy, with a bit of social compassion." He was, in fact, confident that "the Public is once again ready to listen to the notions traditionally associated with the Left—social justice, cohesion, equality of opportunity and, above all, community. They do not want to go back; they want to move on" (p. 6).

In his 2010 political memoir referred to earlier, Tony Blair argued that, in order to emphasize the break with the past, it had been essential to come up with an eye-catching slogan for the 1994 Labour Party conference held in Blackpool in October. (It was, after all, at this conference, his first since becoming leader, that Blair first put forward the idea of abandoning Clause Four of the Constitution as the core statement of the Labour Party's philosophy). It was apparently Blair's new press spokesperson Alastair Campbell who invented the phrase "New Labour, New Britain," to be put up in the hall as the "strapline" for the conference. The idea of renaming the party caused considerable unease among members of Blair's inner circle, and many warned that there would be "a dangerous reaction" from delegates in the hall. At one point, there was even talk of a compromise: "new Labour," with no capital N for the word "new"; but Blair was insistent that, only by renaming the party as "New Labour," could they hope to convince people, supporters and opponents alike, that what was being created was something "totally different." In his words: "There was indeed a hostile reaction from some in the Hall, but it was containable, and the impact was massive: an emphatic signal that this was not going to be just a minor refurbishment, but a wholesale renovation" (Blair, 2010, p. 85).

It seems clear that Tony Blair's election as Labour Party leader in July 1994 was indeed a defining moment in the history of the Labour Party; but the precise nature and significance of the reform program rolled out between 1994 and 1997, and then implemented with all manner of modifications between 1997 and 2010, is still a matter of dispute. Was it a cynical abandonment of the party's "social democratic" values for reasons of electoral expediency; or was it a principled and necessary response to the changing needs of a changing society?

From a Socialist standpoint, leading sociologist and political commentator Stuart Hall has argued that Tony Blair was determined from the outset to abandon Labour's historic agenda and to begin the process of reconstructing social democracy as the means by which "a New Labour variant of neoliberalism" could be sold to the party. Borrowing the skills of triangulation from President Bill Clinton (taking ideas from all parts of the political spectrum to make a "Third Way"), Blair's "hybrid," as Hall calls it, "re-articulated social reform, free enterprise and the market." Using the term "modernization" to cover a program of creeping privatization, New Labour effectively repositioned itself from "centre-left" to "centre-right." According to Hall, Blair and his allies believed that the old route to government was "permanently barred," and had been converted "Damascus-like" to neoliberalism and the market. It was really not necessary to talk about "privatizing" health or education or social services; all you had to do was burrow underneath the distinction between state and market. In Hall's words, "outsourcing, value-for-money, and contract-contestability criteria opened one door after another, through which private capital could slip into the public sector and hollow it out from within. This was to mean New Labour adopting market strategies, submitting to competitive discipline, espousing entrepreneurial values and constructing new entrepreneurial subjects" (Hall, 2011, p. 19). New Labour did initiate some important social reforms, including the minimum wage, better health targets, and attempts to reduce child poverty; but there was "a continuous tension between a strident, Fabian, Benthamite tendency to over-regulate and manage on the one hand and, on the other, the ideology of the market, with its demands for de-regulation and its pressure for access to lucrative areas of public life from which it had hitherto been excluded" (p. 20).

As someone who sees himself as very much subscribing to the social democratic tradition within the Labour Party, former deputy leader Roy Hattersley (1983–1992) has also been very critical of the new direction that the party took under Tony Blair in the 1990s. In an article published in *The Political Quarterly* toward the end of 2011, Hattersley (and his coauthor Kevin Hickson) argued that the Labour Party should have learned to have confidence in the social democratic ideological position that once defined it as a political party. Policy built on a consistent and coherent idea should always have been the preferred option, rather than "grasping at ideas with more news value than substance." In the view of Hattersley and Hickson, Blair and his allies decided that a choice had to be made "between principle and power", and that, since "opposition equated to impotence," it was plainly necessary to compromise in order to win office. One of New Labour's defining characteristics was "The willingness to jettison 'unelectable' principles and policies in order to get into power." And Blair's strategy was given considerable credibility by the mere fact of the party having suffered the indignity of being out of power for so long. The unexpected defeat in the general election of 1992 was presented as evidence that the electorate would never consider voting in sufficient numbers for an overtly "social democratic" policy platform; and the people advising Blair were openly critical of John Smith's alleged belief that "one more push" would see the Labour Party returned to power at the next election. In their critique of the New Labour position, Hattersley and Hickson cite Robert Worcester's 1999 book *Explaining Labour's Landslide* to argue that, had John Smith lived and had Labour remained true to its principles—particularly with regard to equality and wealth redistribution—the party would still have won a major victory in 1997 (Hattersley and Hickson, 2011, p. 6).

Hattersley's views on the Labour Party's dilemma in 1994 have been subjected to severe criticism by former Blair adviser and then cabinet minister David Miliband. Writing in *New Statesman* in February 2012,

Miliband characterized the former deputy leader as a partisan of something called "Reassurance Labour," a set of beliefs that has always seen the central state as the essential mechanism for furthering social democratic goals, and that has failed to realize that "a central state without the discipline of decentralization is likely to become bureaucratic and out-of-touch." In this article, Miliband totally rejected the view that New Labour's big mistake after 1994 was to abandon principle for reasons of electoral expediency. To impale the Labour Party on the choice of "principle or power" would, in his view, have been "logically as well as politically disastrous." There was, after all, no guarantee that an unregenerate Labour Party could ever again win a general election; and the real lesson of 1992 was that "the Party could not rely on an unpopular government to lose an election and give Labour victory." Starting with the rewriting of Clause Four, it was clearly necessary to revise Labour policy on a number of fronts, the better to fulfill the party's values. In Miliband's words:

> After 1994, we did not say that it was a great pity we had to compromise our principles in order to meet the electorate halfway; we said that it was vital to reform the statement of our principles to reflect what we actually believed. The same was true in a broad range of policy areas, including health, education and crime. We changed our policy, the better to fulfil our values, not abandon them. (Miliband, 2012, p. 25)

The Issue of Selection

Where education was concerned, it was soon clear that Tony Blair had no wish to see Labour complete its program of introducing a nationwide system of comprehensive secondary schools. In his book *A Journey*, he was, in fact, remarkably candid in expressing the hostility he had always felt to the program of change that the Labour government had introduced in the 1960s:

> The way comprehensives were introduced and grammar schools abandoned was pretty close to academic vandalism. And not a great reflection on the Secretaries of State—mainly Labour, but also Tory—who, of course, continued to send their own children to private schools. Not experiencing through their own children the reality of the change, and

hugely egged on by the teaching establishment, they legislated so that grammar schools (selective, but also excellent) were changed into comprehensive schools (non-selective and frequently non-excellent, and, on occasions, truly dire).

Blair went on to argue that comprehensive campaigners in the 1960s had made the totally false assumption that the only reason grammar schools were thought to be "better" was because they were able to be selective, thereby ignoring all their other virtues:

> This is to make the same mistake as when people say that private schools are good just because the parents are middle class and better off and the school's facilities are better: that is to say, they are better, only through privilege and class.... The truth is that both types of school are good for other reasons too. They are independent. They have an acute sense of ethos and identity. They have strong leadership, and heads are actually allowed to lead. They are more flexible. They innovate because no one tells them they can't. They pursue excellence. And—and here is a major factor—they assume that excellence is attainable. In other words, they believe that failure is not inevitable, it is avoidable; and it is their fault if they don't manage to avoid it—not the fault of something called "the system," "the background of the children" or "the inadequacy of the parents." (Blair, 2010, p. 579)

These perspectives on selection and the "merits" of grammar schools articulated by Tony Blair, and referring back to how he really felt when he became Labour Party leader in 1994, were certainly shared at the time by Andrew (now Lord) Adonis, soon to become one of the prime minister's closest advisers and usually credited with being the chief architect of New Labour's Academies Programme, launched in March 2000. In *A Class Act: The Myth of Britain's Classless Society*, which Adonis coauthored with Stephen Pollard and which was published in 1997, it was argued that Labour's comprehensive schools had destroyed the life-chances of large numbers of working-class children:

> Grammar-schools... enabled a large proportion of working-class children to mix with their similarly able middle-class peers.... That is why the divided system which emerged after 1944, and which enshrined the idea of a free grammar-school place for the intellectually able rather than the socially well-connected, was the culmination of the arguments of Socialists such as Sydney Webb and R. H. Tawney. The challenge

for the next generation was to widen access to grammar schools, while extending their ethos and their emphasis on qualifications and standards to the secondary modern sector, thereby emulating the achievements of Germany and Holland in particular, with their technical and vocational schools. The comprehensive revolution, tragically, destroyed much of the excellent, without improving the rest.

Comprehensive schools have largely replaced selection by ability with a form of selection by class and house price. Middle-class children now go to middle-class comprehensives, whose catchment areas comprise middle-class neighbourhoods; while working-class children are mostly left to fester in the inner-city comprehensives their parents cannot afford to move away from.... Far from bringing the classes together, England's state schools...are now a force for rigorous segregation. (Adonis and Pollard, 1997, pp. 54–55)

Interviewed by Fraser Nelson for *The Spectator* in January 2007, Adonis (now an education minister in the House of Lords) was anxious to talk about what he saw as the obvious shortcomings of postwar Labour education policy in robust terms. He denounced what he called "The comprehensive school revolution," which, in his view, "destroyed many excellent schools, without improving the rest." And he said he deplored the end of the grammar schools: a move "carried out in the name of equality, but which merely served to reinforce class divisions." In his view, the reckless closure of grammar schools in the 1960s and 1970s "reinforced and intensified class divisions in this country, without doing anything to help those less well off." He admitted that he had been a fierce opponent of comprehensive schools when he was an education journalist in the 1990s; and he told Fraser Nelson: "I have not changed my mind in ten years." He added: "If I could redo the education policy of the 1960s and 1970s, I'd do it all very differently" (Nelson, 2007).

At the time of John Smith's death in 1994, the shadow education secretary was Ann Taylor, who had taken over the portfolio from Jack Straw in 1992. She had consulted widely on education, and her consultative green paper *Opening Doors to a Learning Society* (Labour Party, 1993) was itself the outcome of a wide-ranging and extensive consultative exercise; but, despite her energy and commitment, she was made to realize, after Smith's death, that her position as Labour's education spokesperson was under threat, largely on account of her broad support for comprehensive education. In the words of Blair's early biographer

Anthony Seldon, education was seen by Blair and his allies as "the main unreconstructed 'Old Labour' area of domestic policy," and Ann Taylor could be depicted as "the embodiment of this 'Old Labour' thinking." According to Seldon, her policy could be dismissed as very much "producer driven" (that is to say, by the teaching unions and, specifically, by the National Union of Teachers), rather than "consumer driven" (that is to say, by the parents) (Seldon, 2004, p. 243).

Writing in the education journal *Forum* in 1994, Ann Taylor argued that her green paper was not "a statement of policies to be imposed by Labour politicians." It was "a statement of principles and values that should guide policy-making to ensure a high-quality education for all." And, most important of all, it was based upon the presupposition that schools matter:

> Schools can make a difference. People's lives can be transformed by them. Each of us knows someone who can show how a set of experiences at school opened up a new career, or pointed them in a new direction. The Labour Party was founded upon the belief that good social policy can intervene in society and improve the lives of everyone. We were also founded on the belief that people can grab hold of their own destiny, and that their lives are not to be "determined" by their genetic or environmental background. (Taylor, 1994, p. 4)

The final version of *Opening Doors to a Learning Society* was published as "A Policy Statement on Education" on July 26, 1994, in time for consideration at the 1994 party conference (Labour Party, 1994). And it began by setting out five "key principles" that should guide education policy making in Britain: access for all, quality and equity, continuity, accountability, and partnership.

Where the question of "access" was concerned, it was argued in the document that education should be about "opening doors and keeping them open as wide as possible for as long as possible." The Labour Party rejected the approach whereby too much of educational provision was "concerned with excluding large numbers of people and providing prizes simply for the few." It was clear that the current system was based on "low expectations" and the assumption that "the vast majority of people lack ability." Labour, on the other hand, believed that "quality education demands comprehensive provision at all stages," and rejected any system in which "a few are selected at the expense of the vast majority." On the issue of "continuity," education should be viewed as "a life-long process" and it should not be "terminated at arbitrary points." Recent legislation had resulted in too much power being concentrated in the hands of the secretary of state; and, while it was the task of the central government to create the framework for education, the local delivery of services must always be "the responsibility of those who are democratically and professionally accountable" (Labour Party, 1994, pp. 4–5).

The document also recognized the need for the education system to respond to "the challenges of technological change and the development of new communications infrastructures." It pointed out that across the globe, governments were exploring how best to "exploit the enormous educational potential of technological developments." And it went on:

> A Labour government will promote the development of new, imaginative methods of delivering educational services and the use of collaborative learning opportunities provided by the new technologies. In addition, we will work to promote the cost-effective use of technology in our schools, stimulate educational access to libraries and databases, and ensure that schools receive equal treatment in the provision of resources for information technology education. (Labour Party, 1994, p. 4)

In the view of Professor Sally Tomlinson, who was a member of Jack Straw's Education Advisory Group between 1990 and 1992 and worked for Ann Taylor from 1992 to 1994, the 1994 policy statement was "a genuine attempt to marry 'Old Labour' beliefs in comprehensive education with new ideas related to pedagogy and the role of teachers—an attempt to champion traditional Labour values in a modern setting" (Tomlinson, 2012). And the agenda set out in the paper was also endorsed by Professor Denis Lawton, who wrote later that the document was "a serious and successful attempt to combine Labour Party ethical values and principles with the needs of a modernizing society" (Lawton, 2005, p. 120).

Yet this enthusiasm for Ann Taylor's work was not shared by the new leader of the Labour Party who made it quite clear, even at the press conference to launch the policy document, that he did not share its general approach. He had already stressed in an interview with George Jones of *The Daily Telegraph*, published on July 26, 1994 under the heading "Blair warns Left to Shed Dogmas," that he was determined to continue the modernization of the Labour Party, and that this meant there could be no going "backwards" in education to "the days before the implementation of the 1988 Education Reform Act" (Jones, 1994). At the press conference, he emphasized the need to raise standards in state education; and he was careful to avoid endorsing traditional party pledges to abolish the existing grammar schools in England and Wales and limit financial help for the independent sector (reported in *The Guardian*, July 27, 1994).

At the October 1994 party conference held in Blackpool, Tony Blair and Ann Taylor avoided making specific policy promises, and said nothing about what would happen to the Conservatives' grant-maintained schools under a Labour government, or about whether or not the party would abolish school examination league tables and national testing at 7, 11, and 14. The party leader did claim that education would be "the passion of his administration," and that he would not "tolerate children going to run-down schools, with bad discipline, low standards, mediocre expectations or poor teachers." He went on: "If schools are bad, then they should be made to be good. And if teachers can't teach, then they shouldn't be teaching at all" (reported in *The Times Educational Supplement*, October 7, 1994).

Journalists attending the conference were left in no doubt that Ann Taylor would be "vulnerable" in any reshuffle following forthcoming elections to the shadow cabinet. As it happened, she was soon replaced by David Blunkett, who was quite prepared to rethink Labour's education policy, and whose own somewhat low opinion of the teaching establishment in general, and of the National Union of Teachers in particular, was at least partly shaped by his unhappy experience as a frustrated blind pupil in the state system. In an *Observer* profile published at the end of October, he was described as having "very little sympathy with 'progressive' educational theories" and as being "a strong believer in 'old-fashioned' discipline."

It was argued that he was set to "bury Labour's image as the party of the monolithic comprehensive school, always ready to make excuses for poor schools and bad teachers." He would "welcome greater diversity in schools, back moves to weed out weak teachers and accept the need for regular testing and strict homework policies" (Hugill, 1994). One of his first actions was to announce, on November 20, that a Labour government would publish league tables of schools' examination results.

One of the key figures who now became involved in the development of New Labour education policy was David Miliband, who had been recruited from the Left-of-Centre IPPR (Institute for Public Policy Research) to head the new prime minister's Policy Unit in Downing Street on July 22, 1994. He was the 29-year-old son of the distinguished Marxist intellectual and political theorist Ralph Miliband, author of *The State in Capitalist Society* quoted in chapter 2 who had died earlier in the year; and his brother Ed already worked for Harriet Harman, shadow chief secretary to the Treasury. He was described by Donald Macintyre in *The Independent* as "A leading academic with an outstanding record of original thinking" (Macintyre, 1994) and by Ian Katz in *The Guardian* as someone whose political ideas "crystallized far to the Right of his father's, since he had no wish to follow in his father's footsteps to political irrelevance" (Katz, 1994). David Miliband has sometimes been credited in newspaper articles with drafting New Labour education policy in the mid-1990s, but, interviewed in August 2004, he was anxious to deny that he was the sole or even the principal author of education policy after 1994, emphasizing that he was always happy to work as a member of a team:

> As far as my role was concerned, I worked closely with David Blunkett, the Shadow Education Secretary, Conor Ryan, Blunkett's education adviser, and Michael Barber from the Institute of Education, from 1994 onwards, and they were always the key drivers. It wouldn't be right or fair to pretend that I had my hand on the tiller or my foot on the pedal. I like to think that we were a team; and I think they would also say this. (Miliband, 2004)

In January 1995, David Miliband convened a small education seminar for Tony Blair in the leader's office in the House of Commons, attended by David Blunkett, Conor Ryan, and Michael Barber, where Professor Barber presented a paper in which he said that the critical education theme for the Labour Party should be that "standards matter more than structures." This approach was duly adopted by Blair and Blunkett, and it has been argued that it found favor so quickly largely because "it neatly shifted the argument away from the desirability or otherwise of abolishing the remaining grammar schools, and focused instead on the standards that all secondary schools should be achieving, regardless of their status or structure" (see Seldon, 2004, p. 243). It seems that Tony

Blair was hugely impressed by the tone and substance of this seminar and told those present: "I want to be a Prime Minister who has education as the very centre of his agenda" (ibid).

Under Blair and Blunkett, there was to be a new and remarkably fervent commitment to the idea of specialist secondary schools; and ways clearly had to be found of continuing with the Conservatives' specialist and grant-maintained schools, but under more acceptable guises. The very first "New Labour" document on education, published in June 1995, had the very meaningful title *Diversity and Excellence: A New Partnership for Schools* (Labour Party, 1995), which would not have seemed out of place heading a Conservative education white paper. It proposed that in future all existing categories of state schools should be replaced by just three types of schools:

- community schools, very similar to those whose assets were currently owned by the LEA;
- aided schools, which would be the present church schools (voluntary-aided and voluntary-controlled); and
- foundation schools, which would offer "a new bridge between the powers available to secular and church schools."

It was anticipated that foundation-school status would have special attraction for many, if not all, grant-maintained schools, specialist schools, and CTCs. Such foundation schools would be given powers to employ staff in line with current practice in aided schools, while maintaining national pay and conditions, and would not necessarily be subject to the same admissions policies as those operating in community schools. It was also argued:

> Each of the options listed above would be open to all schools to choose. Schools would be offered the chance to ballot their parents about the precise designation and future of their school. Such ballots would help the governors to decide on which of the three options was best suited to their school, wherever disagreement was clearly expressed amongst the parents. (Labour Party, 1995, pp. 15–16)

The 1995 document also dealt with the vexed question of what to do with the remaining 163 grammar schools. It reiterated Labour's commitment to lifelong learning and comprehensive education, but also made it clear that a future Labour government would not deal with the grammar schools as an issue of national policy. In the words of the document:

> Our opposition to academic selection at 11 has always been quite clear. But while we have never supported grammar schools in their exclusion of children by examination, change can come only through local agreement. Such a change in the character of a school could follow only a clear demonstration of support from the parents affected by such a decision. (Labour Party, 1995, p. 11)

Diversity and Excellence was criticized by a number of commentators (see, for example, Chitty, 1995; Stevenson, 1996; Hatcher, 1997) on the grounds that it was clearly sanctioning different types of secondary schools in a state system where the obsession with choice and diversity—particularly in the large cities—already worked to the benefit of the privileged and the articulate at the expense of the vast majority of working-class and minority ethnic children. Writing in *The Independent* in June 1995, former Labour Party deputy leader Roy Hattersley argued that "by building its policy around different classes of school, Labour is clearly endorsing selection." And he also made the significant point that "once a hierarchy of secondary schools is established, those perceived as 'best' always receive more than their proper share of national resources" (Hattersley, 1995). This sort of criticism greatly angered David Blunkett, who argued that he had inherited a situation that was "frankly bizarre." Previous policy statements had, in his view, "talked vaguely about a local democratic framework," but had "ducked the key issues surrounding selection and admissions policies." His document, on the other hand, did at least aim to formulate "a workable administrative framework for the future" (Blunkett, 1995).

Not surprisingly, the formula for dealing with the remaining grammar schools put forward in *Diversity and Excellence* infuriated many of the more radical and left-wing delegates to the October 1995 Labour Party conference. Accordingly, in his reply to the somewhat acrimonious debate held on October 4, Blunkett sought to placate his skeptical audience by emphasizing: "Read my lips. No selection, either by examination or interview, under a Labour government." The strategy worked, and a revolt, organized around demands for the remaining

163 grammar schools to be incorporated into the comprehensive system, collapsed—on the clear understanding that its chief purpose had already been achieved.

Yet, in the months that followed, it became increasingly clear that "no selection" actually meant "no further selection," and that when David Blunkett began using this new phrase in speeches and media interviews, he was not guilty of a simple "slip of the tongue": he was, in fact, announcing a change of official education policy. The phrase "No selection under a Labour government" signified an end to the existing grammar schools; the phrase "No further selection" was surely a guarantee of their retention. Writing in *The Guardian* at the end of November 1997, Roy Hattersley claimed that this broken promise was "a clear illustration of the contempt for intellectual integrity which characterized New Labour education policy." In Hattersley's words, "David Blunkett made a specific pledge to see him through a difficult party conference, knowing full well that it was not party policy and that Tony Blair would not allow him to honour it" (Hattersley, 1997). But the new education secretary repudiated this charge when he appeared on the BBC Television *Breakfast with Frost* program on November 30, 1997, protesting that when he had used the words "no selection" in the 1995 debate, he had actually intended them to mean "no further selection." There had, therefore, been no change of policy.

Then, in a well-publicized interview with *The Sunday Telegraph* on March 12, 2000, David Blunkett claimed that his 1995 "Read my lips" selection pledge was simply a joke. There was really no need for people to take it all so seriously:

> The 1995 Conference Debate amuses me now because people haven't got the joke. I was obviously parodying George Bush. The Conference laughed at the time; but, since then, nobody has got it. Watch my lips was a joke. As for all the fuss about the "selection" part, if I were doing it again, I would obviously say: "no more selection under a Labour government."

In this important interview, to which we will return in the next chapter, David Blunkett left his readers in no doubt that it was time to "bury the dated arguments of previous decades" and reverse "the outright opposition to grammar schools" that had been "a touchstone of Labour politics for at least 35 years."

Intellectual Preparations for Government

David Miliband has argued (Miliband, 2004) that, under his leadership, the Policy Unit in Downing Street did not really need to look for advice or ideas from other think tanks, pressure groups or "the world of academia," since, in preparing for government, "we had a full education programme; we were not in the business of casting around for ideas." The first education white paper of the Blair government, *Excellence in Schools,* to be discussed fully in the next chapter, was, for example, drafted in the unit before the 1997 general election brought New Labour to power. At the same time, it is true that a number of important books were written between 1994 and 1997, which put forward ideas that found their way into the Labour Party's education program. The somewhat ambiguous catchphrase "Standards not structures," already used by Professor Michael Barber in the 1995 seminar referred to earlier, and which was to be an important theme of the 1997 white paper, also featured prominently in the first edition of *The Blair Revolution: Can New Labour Deliver?* coauthored by Peter Mandelson and Roger Liddle, published in May 1996. It was in this provocative book that Mandelson and Liddle set much of the tone of New Labour's education agenda, arguing that a preoccupation with "structure" in education had absorbed a great deal of energy in the past to little effect, and that the first priority of a Blair administration must be to raise general educational standards in all types of school:

> New Labour now believes that, throughout schooling, standards are clearly more important than structures. Each school should be made clearly responsible for its own performance—and be subject to a mixture of external pressure and support in order to raise it. Performance must be regularly assessed in objective terms that parents can understand so that the school can be compared with elsewhere.... Bad schools should be closed—to be reopened with new management and staff. There should be zero tolerance of failure.... New Labour must now spell out with much greater clarity what its new educational policies mean in practice, and how its new emphasis on standards, not structures, can, in time, transform state education in this country.... There is no good reason why any school in any area should be a failure. (Mandelson and Liddle, 1996, pp. 92–93)

Another important text was *The Learning Game: Arguments for an Education Revolution* by Michael Barber, also first published in 1996, described by Tony Blair on the front cover as "provocative and timely, illuminating and optimistic." From this book, we get the white paper idea that "intervention in schools should be in inverse proportion to success." According to Professor Barber:

> The general assumption behind this principle is that most schools have within them the capacity to improve themselves steadily, as long as National Government provides a sensible policy and funding framework. The precise nature of the intervention in a school which is not succeeding should depend on the extent and character of its failure. (Barber, 1996, p. 149)

In his influential book *The State We're In*, first published in 1995, the leading economist Will Hutton, at that time economics editor of *The Guardian*, argued that only the revival of grammar schools would enable the state system to win back the support of large sections of the middle and professional classes who now sent their children to fee-paying schools:

> Grammar schools and grammar-school streams in comprehensive schools need to be revived in order to attract members of the middle class back to the state system.... The promotion of grammar schools may well be seen as divisive and may also seem a surrender to middle-class aspirations and values; but this is surely better than condemning public institutions to the second-class status that a middle-class exodus from them implies. (Hutton, 1995, p, 311)

According to Anthony Seldon, "Tony Blair became enamoured by Hutton's writing," and found his views on state education "very persuasive" (Seldon, 2004, p. 241). They were certainly views which influenced New Labour in the early years.

Conclusion

This chapter has argued that the election of Tony Blair as Labour Party leader in July 1994, and the subsequent creation of New Labour, were key events in the development or evolution of the party's education policy, signifying, in particular, a refusal to endorse an undiluted commitment to the comprehensive principle at the secondary level. But we have also seen, in chapter 3, that the party has never in its history been clear about the exact meaning of the concept of "secondary education for all." This makes it difficult to claim that Blair and his allies were reversing a policy that had the unequivocal support of all the leading figures in the party, with many keen to argue that the traditional grammar school had a significant role to play in ensuring middle-class support for the state education system and in facilitating a significant degree of working-class upward mobility

Chapter 5

Choice, Diversity, and Selection: The Steady Abandonment of the Comprehensive Ideal, 1997–2007

Introduction

At the general election held on May 1, 1997, the Labour Party gained a landslide victory, bringing to an end 18 years of Conservative rule in Britain. Securing 43 percent of the national vote, its 419 MPs gave it a House of Commons a majority of 179 over all other parties. With the election of only 165 MPs and the receipt of just 31 percent of the national vote, this was the Conservatives' most depressing performance in a general election since their defeat at the hands of Sir Henry Campbell-Bannerman's Liberal Party in January 1906. While all commentators agreed that the result was a major and largely unforeseen triumph for Tony Blair's New Labour Party, there were conflicting views as to its causes and precise significance. Did it represent a massive endorsement of the policies of a Labour Party that had been radically transformed since the death of John Smith in 1994, or was it simply a decisive rejection of the policies and style of the 1992–97 Major administration that had never recovered from the economic crisis of September 1992 when Britain was forced to leave the Exchange Rate Mechanism?

During the election campaign itself, Tony Blair had repeatedly stressed that "education, education, education" were to be "the top three priorities" of his Labour government, with a special emphasis on improvements in the primary school; and this was also the message that the party was anxious to put across in the 1997 New Labour election manifesto, *Because Britain Deserves Better* (Labour Party, 1997).

The five-page introduction to this manifesto by Tony Blair himself, headed "Britain will be better with New Labour," argued in the very first paragraph that Britain could and must be better, with "better schools, better hospitals, better ways of tackling crime, of building a modern Welfare State, and of equipping ourselves for a new world economy." It went on to make the proud boast that the main reason for creating New Labour was to meet the challenges of "a new and rapidly-changing world", of "a new millennium symbolizing a new era opening up for Britain." It was now the chief purpose of New Labour to give Britain a new political choice: the choice between "a failed Conservative Government, exhausted and divided in everything other than its desire to cling on to power" and "a new and revitalized Labour Party," that had been resolute in "transforming itself into a party of the future." New Labour's vision was one of "national renewal: of a country with drive, purpose and energy." The party would create a Britain "equipped to prosper in a global economy of technological change, with a modernized Welfare State; its politics more accountable, and its people confident of their place in the world." This new dynamic party would be putting forward a detailed program for "a new Centre and Centre-Left politics": a set of proposals in each area of policy offering a new and distinctive approach that differed "both from the solutions of the Old Left and from those of the Conservative Right." This was precisely why New Labour was new. It believed in "the strength of its values," while, at the same time, recognizing that "the policies of 1997 could not be those of 1947, or even of 1967." Where education was concerned, there was to be a strong emphasis on "standards," not "structures," in both the primary and secondary sectors, along with a rejection both of "the idea of a return to the 11-plus examination" and of "the monolithic comprehensive schools that take no account of children's differing abilities." New Labour favored schools which identified "the distinct abilities of individual pupils," and organized them in streamed or setted classes which were designed to "maximize their progress in individual subjects." It was necessary to "modernize the comprehensive principle," learning from the experience of the past 30 years. And the introduction ended with a promise by the Labour leader—as an essential part of the party's new "contract with the people"—that, over the five years of a Labour government, education would indeed be "the number one priority," and that the party would "increase the share of national income spent on education," while decreasing it on "the bills of economic and social failure" (Labour Party, 1997, pp. 1, 2, 3, 5).

The manifesto highlighted six policies as being indicative of New Labour's clear determination to make education its "number one priority":

- A reduction in class sizes to thirty or under for all five, six and seven year-olds.
- The provision of nursery places for all four year-olds.
- An attack on low standards in schools.
- Access for all to computer technology.
- The provision of lifelong learning through the establishment of a new University for Industry.
- Increased spending on education as a direct consequence of a fall in the cost of unemployment (Labour Party, 1997, p. 7).

The education section of the manifesto reiterated New Labour's belief that "standards, more than structures" were "the real key to success." A New Labour administration would never "put dogma before children's education," and therefore there would be no attempt to abolish "good schools," whether in the private or in the state sector. Any changes in the admissions policies of grammar schools would be decided by local parents. Schools that enjoyed "grant-maintained" status would continue to prosper, although under a new system of funding—one that did not discriminate unfairly between schools or between pupils. Church schools would be able to retain their distinctive religious ethos. At the same time, attempts would also be made to "build bridges" across such "education divides" as that between the public and the private sectors. On the other hand, the Conservatives' Assisted Places Scheme, whereby a number of "less well-off parents" were able to claim part or all of the fees at certain independent schools from a special government fund at an estimated cost of £180 million per year, would be phased out in order to reduce class sizes for all five-, six-, and seven-year-olds to 30 or under. As part of a determined attack on "under-achievement" in urban areas, new "education action zones" would be established, charged with the crucial task of developing new and imaginative ways of helping "under-performing schools" in areas of disadvantage. There would henceforth be "zero tolerance" of underachievement; a "failing school," unable or unwilling to improve, would be closed—to be replaced by a new establishment on the same site (Labour Party, 1997, p. 7).

The education section was also carefully worded in such a way as to convey the message that while there would be change under a New Labour government, there would also be continuity and consolidation. And in this regard, it had been emphasized, even before the general election, that in the event of a Labour victory, several key personnel would remain in their posts at the major education quangos: Anthea Millett at the TTA (Teacher Training Agency), Nicholas Tate at the QCA (Qualifications and Curriculum Authority), and Chris Woodhead, a divisive and highly controversial figure commanding very little respect among classroom teachers, at Ofsted (Office for Standards in Education), which had been set up by the 1992 Education (Schools) Act as a new "independent" body responsible for contracting independent teams to inspect all state primary and secondary schools in the country.

The 1997 White Paper and the 1998 Education Act

One of the first measures of the new Blair administration was to implement a promise made in the election manifesto, by introducing a short bill phasing out the Conservatives' Assisted Places Scheme, with the intention of using the money thereby released to reduce the class sizes for five-, six-, and seven-year-olds.

Then, in July, just 67 days after assuming office, the government published an 84-page white paper, *Excellence in Schools*, setting out the education agenda for the lifetime of the parliament. Although many commentators were understandably impressed by the speed with which this white paper was produced, it seems clear from comments by David Miliband cited earlier in this chapter, that many of the ideas which found their way into the document had been worked upon in the Downing Street Policy Unit between 1994 and 1997.

In his Foreword to this document, the new secretary of state David Blunkett stressed the importance of rejecting all the usual excuses for underperformance in schools:

> To overcome economic and social disadvantage and to make equality of opportunity a reality, we must strive to eliminate, and never excuse, under-achievement in the most deprived parts of our country.... Educational attainment encourages aspiration and self-belief in the next generation; and it is through family learning, as well as scholarship through formal schooling, that success will come.... We are talking about investing in human capital in the age of knowledge. And to compete in the global economy, to live in a civilized society, and to develop the talents of each and every one of us, we will have to unlock the potential of every young person. By doing so, each can flourish, building on their own strengths and developing their own special talents. We must now overcome the spiral of disadvantage in which alienation from, or failure within, the education system is passed from one generation to the next. (DfEE, 1997, p. 3)

In the first Chapter, entitled "A New Approach," the white paper listed the SIX principles that would be underpinning New Labour's reform agenda:

- Education will be at the heart of government.
- Policies will be designed to benefit the many, not the few.
- Standards will matter more than structures.
- Intervention in schools will be in inverse proportion to success.
- There will be zero tolerance of under-performance.
- Government will work in partnership with all those committed to raising standards (DfEE, 1997, pp. 11–12)

It was then confidently predicted in this Chapter that by the year 2002:

- There will be a greater awareness across society of the importance of education and increased expectations of what can be achieved.
- Standards of performance will be higher. (DfEE, 1997, p. 14)

A significant part of the white paper was concerned with raising standards of literacy and numeracy in the primary school, with the proposed introduction of a daily Literacy Hour in September 1998 and of a daily Numeracy Hour in September 1999, but there were also a large number of far-reaching proposals affecting the secondary sector:

1. The comprehensive principle would be "modernized," to ensure that all pupils, whatever their talents, would be able to develop their diverse abilities. Comprehensive education would henceforth be expected to provide "a broad, flexible and motivating education," that recognized "the different talents of all children," and delivered "excellence for everyone."
2. The setting of pupils by "ability" should be "the norm" in all secondary schools. Mixed ability grouping had not proved capable of "playing to the strengths of every child," and the Government was not prepared to ignore existing shortcomings and "defend the failings of across-the-board mixed-ability teaching."
3. There would be a pilot program of about 25 Education Action Zones (EAZs), charged with the key task of "motivating young people in tough inner-city areas." These would be phased in over two or three years, and set up in areas with a mixture of "under-performing schools and the highest levels of disadvantage." Each would be expected to operate on the basis of an "action forum," which would include parents and "representatives from the local business and social community," as well as "representatives from the constituent schools and the LEA." A typical Education Action Zone would probably have two or three secondary schools, with supporting primaries and associated SEN (special educational needs) provision.
4. There would be "an extensive network of specialist schools," developing their own distinctive identity and expertise. These would focus on technology, languages, sports, or arts, and should be "a resource for local people and the neighboring schools to draw on." They would be able to give priority to applicants who demonstrated "the relevant aptitude."
5. Every secondary school would be inspected by Ofsted at least once every six years. Between these inspections, the performance of schools would be monitored regularly by LEAs on the basis of objective performance information. By April 1999, each LEA would be working to an Education Development Plan (EDP) agreed with the DfEE and the schools, showing how educational standards in all schools could rise.

6. LEAs would be expected to give early warnings to governors of those schools "causing concern" and then be prepared to intervene if necessary. Where schools showed insufficient evidence of "tangible recovery," it might then be necessary to consider a "fresh start" policy. This "fresh start" could take one or other of a variety of different forms. It could mean closing the school, and transferring all the pupils to nearby "successful" schools. In less extreme cases, it might involve another school taking over the "underperforming" school to "set it on a new path"; or closing the school temporarily and then reopening it on either the same or a different site, but with a new name and under new management.
7. The Department for Education and Employment would be encouraged to become more proactive and outward-looking, through the work of the Standards Task Force (STF) and the Standards and Effectiveness Unit. The STF was intended to promote good practice, and guarantee the "delivery" of literacy and numeracy targets. It had already been established, with the secretary of state as the chair, and with Chris Woodhead, the chief inspector of schools, and Tim Brighouse, the then director of education for Birmingham, as the two vice-chairs. (This was thought at the time to constitute a somewhat "explosive" mixture, Tim Brighouse being viewed as a broadly left-wing defender of LEAs, classroom teachers, and the problems faced by "disadvantaged" pupils; and Chris Woodhead anxious to portray himself as a right-wing critic of LEAs, teachers, and "progressive" teaching methods—see, for example, Carvel (1998). As it happened, the pessimistic forecasts of many commentators proved justified; it was not long before Tim Brighouse felt obliged to resign.) The establishment of the Standards and Effectiveness Unit in the DfEE, headed by Michael Barber, was intended to underline the promise, reiterated several times in the white paper, that "standards" matter more than "structures." Among the tasks of the unit was to promote the use and analysis of performance data to measure pupils' progress at national, local, and school level, and to ensure that the government's new policy of "zero tolerance" of underperformance was applied to all schools.
8. As foreshadowed in the 1995 policy document, *Diversity and Excellence*, there would be three types of secondary schools: community, aided, and foundation. The community schools would

be based on the existing county schools; aided schools would be based on the existing voluntary-aided schools; and foundation schools would offer a sort of "bridge" between the powers available to secular and to church schools. These three categories would embrace all local authority and former grant-maintained schools; and it was anticipated that foundation status would have special attractions for most GM establishments. Unlike community schools, aided and foundation schools could employ their own staff and own their own premises.
9. New national guidelines on school admissions policies would be set by the secretary of state; and aided and foundation schools would be able to put forward their own policies in the light of the DfEE guidelines.
10. Secondary school performance tables would be published to LEAs ahead of national publication, so that they could respond more easily to requests for information from parents when the results were published.
11. Where grammar schools still existed in England, their future would be decided by ballots of eligible local parents, and not by LEAs
12. Ways would be found of creating new partnerships between state and private schools. There should be a more positive contribution from the independent sector toward the government's goal of raising educational standards for all children. (DfEE, 1997)

It is fair to say that the 1997 white paper enjoyed a relatively warm welcome from media commentators, union leaders and parents' organizations. A report in *The Independent*, for example, on July 8, 1997, the day after the white paper was published, declared that "published yesterday, under the banner of 'zero tolerance of failure'," *Excellence in Schools* paved the way for an improved school system in which "tough improvement targets will be set at every level, from the Government through local authorities and schools down to individual teachers" (Ward, 1997). Choosing the headline "Ambitious Plan Excites Teachers," *The Guardian* began its own report on July 8 by claiming that "the Government yesterday won the first round of its battle to raise standards in schools, when the teaching unions and the local education authorities rallied to support a white paper promising hugely ambitious improvement targets and draconian penalties for under-performance" (Carvel and Macleod, 1997). It was reported in the *Guardian* story that Doug McAvoy, the general secretary of the National Union of Teachers, had hailed the white paper's firm commitments on class sizes, particularly for five- to seven-year-olds, along with equitable funding and fair and open admission policies. And David Hart, the general secretary of the National Association of Headteachers, welcomed the pressure that could come from "clear performance targets and the continued publication of league tables." The Labour-dominated Local Government Association welcomed the prospect of new powers to support schools in need of help and called for additional reserve powers to intervene, where necessary, in "failing schools" (Carvel and Macleod, 1997). Yet, while endorsing the idea that in future education policies should be designed to "benefit the many, not the few," the organization CASE (Campaign for State Education) had strong reservations about a number of the white paper's features: namely, the emphasis on "failing schools"; the idea that specialist secondary schools should be encouraged to select pupils on "aptitude"; and the lack of government support for a phasing out of existing grammar schools. A CASE leaflet asked two important questions: "Where is the evidence that there is value in promoting 'diversity' by allowing schools to develop a particular identity, character, and expertise?" and "Why was there a need for three types of state school: community, aided, and foundation?" (CASE, 1997, p. 1).

As we have seen, one of the key themes of both the New Labour election manifesto and the 1997 white paper was that "standards" were more important than "structures"; and in their book *The Blair Revolution: Can New Labour Deliver?* to which reference was made in the previous chapter, Peter Mandelson and Roger Liddle attacked "educational egalitarians" for regarding "the structure of schools as far more important than the quality of what is learned" and for showing "a far greater concern for the social balance of a school's admissions than for the destination of a school's graduates" (Mandelson and Liddle, 1996, p. 91). Yet it can be argued that the use of the term "structure" in this context and in the oft-repeated mantra "Standards not structures," so very evident in *Excellence in Schools*, is both ambiguous and confusing. As I have written elsewhere:

> If the term refers to the structure of the education system as a whole, one is tempted to ask: what sort of national framework would we now

have in Britain if large numbers of parents, teachers, local education authorities, and politicians had not cared about "structure" in the 1950s and 1960s, and campaigned for a comprehensive system of secondary schooling? If it refers to the "structure" of individual schools (which, in any case, cannot be viewed in isolation from the system as a whole), then we are being asked to consider a false dichotomy. Standards and structures are inter-related and can be understood only in relation to each other. A comprehensive school, which is, in reality, a secondary modern school in a still selective local system with inadequate resources to perform a wide variety of tasks, is less likely to achieve excellent results of the kind measured by Ofsted than will another school in the same area, which occupies a safe and privileged position in the local hierarchy of schools. It is one of the major shortcomings of the school improvement movement that it often treats schools as if they operated in some sort of social and political vacuum. And it is one of the shortcomings of the White Paper that it actually ducks many of the key issues concerning structure, selection and admissions criteria. (Chitty, 1997a, p. 71)

The first major education bill of the various Blair administrations, with the legislative proposals based on the reforms outlined in the 1997 white paper, was introduced into parliament in December 1997 and became law in July 1998. In seven parts, it comprised 145 sections and 32 schedules. Bearing in mind the repeated assertion in the white paper that "standards matter more than structures," it seems somewhat ironic that the act was, in fact, chiefly concerned with structure, with 89 of the 145 sections being devoted to the new categories of state maintained schools, their establishment, financing, admissions, and selection arrangements. There was no mention of the comprehensive school as such in the 1998 act.

Excellence in Schools had been anxious to declare support for the previous government's program of specialist schools, and had stipulated that "schools with a specialism will continue to be able to give priority to children who demonstrate the relevant aptitude, as long as that is not misused to select on the basis of 'general academic ability'" (DfEE, 1997, p. 71). Clause 102 of the 1998 School Standards and Framework Act then gave legislative backing to this assurance by stating that a maintained secondary school may "make provision for the selection of pupils for admission to the school by reference to their 'aptitude' for one or more prescribed subjects" where:

- the admission authority for the school are satisfied that the school has a specialism in the subject or subjects in question; and
- the proportion of selective admissions in any relevant age group does not exceed 10 percent.

It has to be admitted that this provision in the 1998 act caused very real disquiet among many teachers and educationists who argued that in a class-divided and highly competitive society, different school specialisms could never enjoy equal status and would rapidly become ranked in a hierarchy of status. At the same time, the government's long-term plans seemed to be based on the confident but false assumption that children could actually be tested for "particular talents," rather than for "general ability"; whereas it was not really clear what "aptitude" or "talent" meant in this context, or how it could be distinguished from "general ability." Writing in *Education Guardian* in March 1998, Professor Peter Mortimore, the then director of the Institute of Education in London, argued that the government's thinking seemed to fly in the face of the large body of existing research evidence:

> While the theory behind the creation of specialist schools might indeed be worthy, seeking to achieve it by allowing ten percent selection is simply misguided.... It assumes that children can be tested for "particular talents," rather than for "general ability"; while the large body of research evidence suggests otherwise.... Except in music and perhaps art, it does not seem possible to diagnose specific aptitudes for most school curriculum subjects. Instead, what emerges from such testing is a general ability to learn, which is often, but not always, associated with the advantages of coming from a middle-class home. How can headteachers know if the "aptitude" of a ten-year-old in German shows anything more that their parents' ability to pay for extra language lessons. (Mortimore, 1998)

The Government was not inclined to take note of such reservations, and when a further 51 specialist schools were named in June 1998, bringing the total to over three hundred or around one in ten of England's secondary schools, Education Minister Estelle Morris was keen to announce a broader remit for these new schools:

> Specialist schools and colleges will have a key contribution to make in raising standards and delivering excellence in schools.... They will help

thousands of young people to learn new skills and thereby progress into employment, further training and higher education, according to their individual abilities, aptitudes, and ambitions. (Quoted in *The Evening Standard*, June 16, 1998)

And finally, in an interview with David Frost on the BBC Television's *Breakfast with Frost* program broadcast on January 16, 2000, Prime Minister Tony Blair was excited to announce that hundreds of comprehensive schools would be turned into specialist colleges over the next three years, as the government decided to divert its main focus from primary to secondary education. It was clear that the government was now on target to have five hundred in place by September 2000, and eight hundred by September 2003, which meant that, by then, nearly one in four state secondary schools in England and Wales would have a specialism in technology, languages, sport, or the creative arts. Schools could achieve "specialist status" by raising £50,000 in business sponsorship, setting realizable but ambitious improvement targets and involving the local community. In return, they would receive a £100,000 capital grant and an extra £120 per pupil for at least four years.

Selection, Diversity and Specialization: The Comprehensive School under Threat

After nearly three years in government, Tony Blair's education ministers were prepared to acknowledge that arguments about 11-plus selection and the future of the grammar schools were part of a faded agenda and no longer worth engaging with. In an interview with *The Sunday Telegraph* in March 2000 where, as we saw in the previous chapter, Education Secretary David Blunkett denied that he had ever meant to promise that there would be "no selection under a Labour government," he also announced that "Labour's war against grammars is over." He said that it was time to "bury the dated arguments of previous decades" and "reverse the outright opposition to grammar schools" that had been "a touchstone of Labour politics for at least 35 years." He went on:

> I'm not interested in hunting the remaining grammar schools.... I'm desperately trying to avoid returning to the whole debate in education as it was in the 1960s and 1970s, concentrating on the issue of selection,

when it should be concentrating on the raising of standards in all schools.... The arguments about selection are part of a past agenda. We have set up a new system which says "if you don't like grammar schools, you can get rid of them"; but this really isn't the key issue for the year 2000. The real issue is what we are going to do about the whole of secondary education.... There are only 163 grammar schools—let's get on with the job of giving a decent education to all our kids.... If all future attempts to close grammar schools fail, I shall feel totally vindicated. (*The Sunday Telegraph*, March 12, 2000)

The final comment in this revealing interview referred to the announcement two days earlier (March 10) of the voting figures in the very first ballot on the future of a grammar school, held as a result of the government's policy of leaving the future of 11-plus selection in the hands of local parents. The long-term future of Ripon Grammar School in north Yorkshire, founded in 1556, and one of the oldest in England, was guaranteed as parents decided by a clear majority of around two to one to reject the proposition that henceforth the school be required to admit children "of all abilities." On a 75 percent turnout, 1.493 of the 3,000 parents, who were entitled to vote because their children attended one or other of 14 "feeder" state primary or independent preparatory schools, voted to reject the proposition, with only 748 voting in favor. This majority was so decisive that the pro-comprehensive "lobby" decided immediately to abandon plans to challenge the result, but the Ripon branch of the Campaign for State Education (CASE) did complain that more than 25 percent of the parents eligible to vote came from outside the area, while a similar proportion educated their primary-age children in the independent sector. It was also considered significant that the secondary modern school in Ripon had recently been "upgraded" by being given "specialist school" status. Responding to the Ripon voting figures, Education Minister Estelle Morris saw no need to take account of the various "anomalies" highlighted by CASE:

> The Government respects the decision of parents to retain the current admission arrangements at Ripon Grammar School.... At all stages of the debate, the decision has been a matter for the parents, and they have all had the chance to express their views. (Reported in *The Daily Telegraph*, March 11, 2000)

In the light of this setback in Yorkshire, and of a distinct lack of encouragement from the government, it is hardly surprising that no other groups of parents in other parts of the country were prepared to risk wasting time and money on a similar enterprise in the future.

March 2000 was to prove a hectic month for the Department of Education and Employment, with the announcement of a number of initiatives that were to have far-reaching implications for the future of the education system. In a well-publicized speech at a National Union of Teachers conference on secondary education held on March 1, David Blunkett had warned that poverty would no longer be acceptable as an excuse for failure and underachievement:

> There are cynics out there who say that school performance is all about socio-economics and the areas where "failing" schools are located. In fact, no child is pre-ordained by their class, gender, ethnic group or home life to fail.... I can't "bus" children from one end of a city to another; but I can do something to spread what is working. I can bring in to schools, which are clearly not succeeding, "inspirational" headteachers who have made education work elsewhere. (Reported in *The Guardian*, March 2, 2000)

In David Blunkett's view, it was unacceptable that there were 86 secondary schools with fewer than 15 percent of pupils gaining at least five "good" GCSE passes at grade C or above and as many as 530 schools with a current pass rate below 25 percent. Local authorities would now be asked to consider a "fresh start" for all those secondary schools where fewer that 15 percent of GCSE candidates managed five good (A to C) passes for three years in a row. He went on to announce three targets to secure "rapid improvement" in the secondary sector:

1. By 2003, all secondary schools must secure a pass rate of at least 15 percent of students gaining five good GCSE passes;
2. By 2004, there should be no secondary school with a pass rate below 20 percent;
3. By 2006, all secondary schools should gain a pass rate of at least 25 percent. (Reported in *The Guardian*, March 2, 2000)

These targets were reiterated in the 2001 green paper *Schools: Building on Success: Raising Standards, Promoting Diversity, Achieving Results* (DfEE, 2001).

Also in March 2000, David Blunkett launched the City Academies Programme. Conceived as "a radical approach" to breaking "the cycle of under-performance and low expectations" in inner-city schools, and clearly modeled on the Conservatives' City Technology Colleges Project, this radical new venture was intended to enable rich sponsors from the private and voluntary sectors to establish new schools in challenging locations, whose basic running costs would then be met fully by the state. Since it can be viewed as a highly significant privatizing measure, it will be dealt with at length in the next chapter.

In the years following 2000, and particularly while Tony Blair was in office, speeches by the prime minister and his education ministers, and government green and white papers and the legislation based upon them revealed a growing disillusionment with the concept of the comprehensive school and a determination to bring greater diversity to an already diverse and fragmented education system, particularly at the secondary level. By the time David Blunkett left office in June 2001, there was a hierarchy of at least 16 types of secondary schools, each with its own legal status and unique admission procedures:

- private (independent) schools
- city technology colleges
- city academies
- grammar schools
- foundation specialist schools
- voluntary specialist schools
- community specialist schools
- beacon schools
- foundation schools
- voluntary aided schools
- voluntary controlled schools
- community schools
- foundation special schools
- community special schools
- Pupil Referral Units
- Learning Support Centers

Between 2001 and 2007, a number of government publications, and the publicity surrounding them, seemed designed to antagonize all those who failed to see the merits of greater diversity at the secondary level, and who wished instead to champion the cause of a more unified education system. The Blair government was clearly prepared to exploit a perceived concern about low standards in parts of the system; and it is interesting to note that much of the reaction to the green paper *Schools: Building on Success: Raising Standards, Promoting Diversity, Achieving Results*, published in February 2001 (and referred to in a previous paragraph), concentrated on its hostile attitude toward the concept of the traditional comprehensive school, with commentators taking note of David Blunkett's comment in the Introduction that such schools often failed to identify and provide for "the talents of each individual pupil, not least those with high academic abilities, and those requiring a high-quality vocational or work-related route post-14" (DfEE, 2001, p. 5). Many of the reporters present at the official press launch held on February 12, 2001 were somewhat taken aback by the failure of the prime minister to distance himself from the deliberate and insulting claim made by his official spokesperson, Alastair Campbell, that "the day of the bog-standard comprehensive" was clearly over. And it could be argued that by heralding "a post-comprehensive era of secondary education," Tony Blair was himself providing ammunition for the enemies of the comprehensive reform, provoking such headlines in the right-wing press as "Comprehensives Have Failed, Says Blair" in *The Daily Telegraph* (February 13, 2001) and "Death of the Comprehensive" in *The Daily Mail* (February 13, 2001). According to the prime minister, "Diversity must now become the norm, not the exception."

Transforming secondary education was certainly the declared mission of the Blair government in 2001; this was, in fact, the title of Chapter 4 of the February green paper. In this respect, it is possible to identify three major themes and policy alignments that dominate this important Chapter:

- a rejection of the principles underpinning the era of the "one size fits all" comprehensive school (though it is, of course, debatable whether such an era ever actually existed);
- a concern to see the promotion of greater diversity among secondary schools and the extension of "autonomy" for "successful" schools;
- a desire to see private and voluntary sector sponsors play a greater role in the provision of secondary schooling.

According to the green paper, it was necessary to modernize the comprehensive model, in order to prevent "parents with increasing income in the most prosperous parts of the country" turning to private schools as the only means of securing a decent education for their children. If this were to happen on a large scale, "growing numbers of people would become less willing to pay taxes to fund public education, which would then decline in quality and be there only for the disadvantaged" (DfEE, 2001, p. 8).

As an important means of "promoting diversity" in the system, the government intended to accelerate the Specialist Schools Programme, so that there would be around 1,000 specialist secondary schools in operation by September 2003, and 1,500 by September 2006. In addition to an increase in the number of such schools, there would also be an extension of the range of specialisms available. It was already possible for schools to specialize in technology, modern languages, sports, and the arts, and it would now be possible to opt for one of three new specialist areas: engineering, science, and business and enterprise. Business and enterprise schools would be encouraged to develop strong links with local businesses, and to develop teaching skills in business studies, financial literacy, and enterprise-related vocational programs.

There would also be a new category of advanced specialist schools, which would be open to "high-performing" secondary schools after operating for five years as specialist schools. Such schools could volunteer to take on a number of innovative curriculum ideas from a "menu," drawn up centrally by the government. In return, they could receive an additional capital investment to strengthen their role as "centers of excellence." An important part of their work might also be initial teacher training, working in collaboration with university departments of education.

David Blunkett had already announced, in March 1999, that there was to be a new category of beacon schools, designed to develop and spread "good practice" among neighboring establishments. It was now planned that there would be around 1,000 Beacon Schools by September 2001, including some 250 at secondary level.

Faith-based schools would also play a prominent role in the government's new diverse education system. There were already 560 secondary schools provided by the Church of England or the Catholic church; and the Government wished to see more Muslim, Sikh, and Greek Orthodox schools brought inside the state system and funded on the same basis as existing "aided" schools.

While there was much enthusiasm for the City Academies Programme launched in March 2000, comparatively little space was accorded in the new green paper to the Education Action Zones initiative which had occupied such a prominent place in the *Excellence in Schools* white paper back in 1997.

Many of the themes and policy initiatives outlined in the 2001 green paper were reiterated and expanded upon later in the year, in a white paper *Schools Achieving Success*, published by the new department for Education and Skills (DfES) on September 5, 2001 just three months after Tony Blair's (second) resounding victory in the June general election that gave New Labour 42 percent of the national vote and a majority over all other parties in the House of Commons of 167. The main proposals found their way into a new education bill, published on November 23, which, in turn, served as the basis for the 2002 Education Act, which received the royal assent on July 24, 2002.

By the time the white paper was published, David Blunkett had moved to the Home Office and been replaced as education secretary by Estelle Morris; but this change was of no consequence as far as education policy was concerned. In the space of a short three-page introduction, the word "diversity" appeared no less than seven times, invariably linked with such terms as "devolution," "autonomy," or "flexibility." In the words of the officials who drafted the document, "devolution and diversity" were the "essential hallmarks of the White Paper"; "Ours is a vision of a school system, which values opportunity for all, and embraces diversity and autonomy as the means to achieve it"; it is time to embrace "flexibility and diversity," and to move away from "the outdated argument about diversity versus uniformity" (DfES, 2001, pp. 1–3).

Chapter 5 was called "Excellence, Innovation and Diversity," and it began by announcing that "we want to build a flexible and diverse education system in which every secondary school is excellent and plays to its strengths; where schools learn from one another; are freed to innovate; and where the best schools lead the system" (DfES, 2001, p. 37). There would be at least 1,000 specialist schools in operation by September 2003 and at least 1,500 by the year 2005, this latter date being a year earlier than the target date put forward in the green paper. In addition to the new specialisms on offer in engineering, science, and business and enterprise, there would now be a fourth: mathematics and computing. The number of Beacon Schools in existence in September

2001—around 1,000—already included some 250 secondary schools; and the government was committed to expanding the number to at least 400 by the year 2005.

Education Action Zones were barely mentioned in the white paper; but the authors were anxious to highlight the Excellence in Cities (EiC) Programme, which had been launched in March 1999, and which was designed to raise levels of achievement in all urban schools by targeting extra resources in areas of need. Reports which appeared in the national press in the Autumn of 2001 to the effect that the EAZ Plan was being dropped were hotly denied by a number of the leading zone directors; but in November 2001, the schools minister Stephen Timms told a conference of zone directors that none of the contracts for the existing 73 zones would be renewed when they expired at the end of their five-year period, and that the more successful EAZ experiments would simply be incorporated within the Excellence in Cities Programme (reported in *The Times Educational Supplement*, November 16, 2001).

The white paper announced the establishment of a new Academy for Gifted and Talented Youth to further the interests of "gifted and talented" pupils. This would be based in a university, and would seek to support schools, by running summer schools that were able to offer the sort of "fast-paced, advanced and flexible courses" that could not normally be found in state secondary schools. In the meantime, schools would be expected to identify pupils with "outstanding academic ability" and consider "express sets, fast-tracking, and early entry to GCSE and advanced qualifications" (p. 21). At the same time, grammar schools and nonselective schools should be encouraged to work closely together to give the most able pupils "the targeted support they need." In a press release issued in December 2001, Stephen Timms announced the funding of 28 school partnerships, designed to "break down perceived barriers between the sectors" by "sharing resources and raising academic standards":

> The time of the "one-size-fits-all" approach to secondary education in this country has long gone. We now have a mature understanding of all the benefits of a diverse system, tailored to meet the needs of every pupil in every town. But we must ensure that best practice is spread throughout the system to everyone's benefit.... There is a wealth of talent and expertise in both the grammar and non-selective sectors—and we want to unlock the potential for both sectors to share that knowledge. These

unique partnerships I am announcing today will allow selective and non-selective schools to build new relationships—between both pupils and staff—and raise standards for all. (Timms, 2001)

The idea that we had to move away from the concept of the "one-size-fits-all" comprehensive was a prominent theme of an article that Estelle Morris wrote for *The Observer* on June 23, 2002, and of a speech she delivered the following day to the Social Market Foundation. In her wide-ranging *Observer* piece, Ms. Morris argued that while comprehensive education could claim many successes, it now had to be "modernized" to take account of a changing society. In the pursuit of "opportunity for all," comprehensive schools had concentrated on developing their "essential sameness," and had failed to offer children an education "tailored to individual needs." She went on:

> Comprehensive schools don't cherish their differences. Yet equality of opportunity will never be achieved by giving all children the same basic education. It is achieved by tailoring education to the needs of the individual. The old tripartite system could never have done that. Comprehensive schools could, but so far haven't. In the fight for equal opportunity, we may have emphasized the "equality" too much, and the "opportunity" too little. This is characterized in our attitude to excellence. Too often, it is confused with "elitism," and with the failure to understand that recognizing and celebrating those who achieve does not hold back others.... We must obviously keep the entitlement curriculum that comprehensive education offers all children. But we also have to encourage every single one of our secondary schools to develop their own sense of mission and play to their strengths. That is why we will invest in specialist schools and training schools, Beacon Schools and City Academies, each school choosing its own identity within the comprehensive family. We have to get away from the perception that one size fits all schools and the concept of "ready-to-wear, off-the-shelf comprehensives." (Morris, 2002b)

In the speech itself, delivered on June 24, 2002, the education secretary reiterated many of these themes, arguing that the comprehensive system had failed in its mission to "raise standards for all," and that it was now time to end the era of the "one-size-fits-all" comprehensive school, by promoting greater diversity within the system—particularly through the spread of specialist schools and city academies. Schools had to be "modernized," by offering children a specialist form of education, "tailored to individual needs." The "comprehensive ideal" would "wither and die," unless schools embraced the government's agenda for change. Interesting and controversial though these comments were, it was, in fact, an ill-judged, unscripted aside that dominated newspaper reports on June 25. Ms. Morris felt she could say, "I know that all secondary schools are not identical. As a former teacher myself, I go into some schools and think: 'I would like to work here'; but there are some, I simply wouldn't touch with a bargepole." Not surprisingly, these remarks angered the majority of the teacher unions, reminding them of Alastair Campbell's 2001 "bog-standard comprehensive" jibe, and prompting such headlines as: "Morris Infuriates Teachers with Bargepole Insult" in *The Times*, and "Bargepole Jibe Angers Teachers" in *The Guardian*. In the view of John Dunford, general secretary of the Secondary Heads Association: "Estelle Morris has demonstrated that she is on-message with 10 Downing Street, but miles off-message with the teaching force to which we expect her to give supportive leadership." And Doug McAvoy, leader of the National Union of Teachers was even more outspoken: "This is an outrageous statement which ill becomes the Secretary of State for Education. There will be many teachers wondering whether they are teaching in a school she wouldn't touch with a bargepole, and her statement will leave them asking the obvious question—If she would not teach here, why should they?" (Reported in *The Times*, June 25, 2002)

In his speech to the October 2002 Labour Party conference held in Blackpool, Tony Blair repeated all the criticisms of schools made by his education ministers, and suggested that the days of the typical comprehensive school were now over. "We need to move on to the post-comprehensive era," he declared, "where schools may keep the principle of 'equality of opportunity,' but where we open up the system to new and different ways of education, built round the needs of the individual child" (reported in *The Times*, October 2, 2002). And in a speech to a specialist schools conference held in Birmingham at the end of November 2002, the prime minister defended his education policies against charges that the government was, in effect, creating a two-tier education system. He characterized the Left as that body of individuals who "mistook uniformity as the only guarantee of equality." Britain was now moving to "a post one-size-fits-all" comprehensive era, where there was "diversity, different types of school and the freedom to innovate"— all with the goal of "creating more good secondary schools in every local community." An escalator of schools would give every child a fair chance. The government's reform agenda was not "the enemy of social justice and educational advance," but "the route to achieve it" (reported in *The Daily Telegraph*, November 27, 2002).

A Five Year Strategy for Children and Learners, published by the Department for Education and Skills on July 8, 2004, during Charles Clarke's period as education secretary (October 2002—December 2004), argued that the "central characteristic" of the new and modernized education system, which the government was planning, would be "personalization"—"so that the system fits to the individual, rather than the individual having to fit to the system." The corollary of this was that the system had to be "both freer and more diverse"—with "more flexibility to help meet individual needs," and "more choices between courses and types of provider," so that there really would be "different and personalized opportunities available" (DfES, 2004a, p. 4).

This 110-page document listed the five principles of reform that would now underpin "the drive for a step change in children's services, education and training":

1. Greater personalization and choice, with the wishes and needs of children's services, parents and learners centre-stage.
2. The opening up of services to new and different providers leading to new ways of delivering services.
3. Freedom and independence for frontline headteachers, governors, and managers, with clear simple "accountabilities" and more secure streamlined funding arrangements.
4. A major commitment to staff development, with high quality support and training to improve assessment, care, and teaching.
5. Partnerships with parents, employers, volunteers, and voluntary organizations to maximize the life chances of children, young people, and adults. (DfES, 2004a, p. 7)

One of the most controversial and far-reaching proposals in this 2004 strategy was the idea of setting up a network of "independent specialist schools," to replace "traditional comprehensives"—described in the document as "a decisive system-wide advance" (p. 8). Chapter 4 was actually headed "Independent Specialist Schools," and began by announcing that the government now had two goals: more choice for parents and pupils; and independence for schools. To achieve these two goals, there would be an increase in the number of two types of schools: specialist schools and City Academies. The number of specialist schools had already increased from 196 when New Labour came to power in 1997, to 1,955 as the projected figure for September 2004; there were plans for a further massive increase over the next four years. There were now ten specialisms on offer, with technology proving the most popular (545 schools), followed by arts (305), sports (283), science (224), languages (203), maths and computing (153), and business and enterprise (146). It was possible for schools offering technology, arts, sports, modern languages, and music to select up to 10 percent of their pupils on the basis of their proven "aptitude" for the subject (p. 47). Alongside this development, it was envisaged that the number of City Academies—just 17 in September 2004—would have increased to at least 200 by the year 2010. It was further intended that 95 percent of all state secondaries would be either independent specialist schools or City Academies by the year 2008 (p. 56).

The 2005 White Paper and the 2006 Education Act

The culmination of Tony Blair's plans to modernize and reorganize the education system were the proposals outlined in the 2005 white paper *Higher Standards, Better Schools for All: More Choice for Parents and Pupils*, which, in turn, served as the basis for the provisions of the 2006 Education and Inspections Bill. The radical nature of the new plans served to alienate a large body of opinion within the Labour Party, both inside and outside parliament; and it is fair to say that Education Secretary Ruth Kelly, who had taken over the post from Charles Clarke in December 2004, found it difficult to mount a coherent defense of the government's broad agenda.

Tony Blair had secured a third successive general election victory in May 2005, and a reduced Commons victory of just 67 was in no way meant to signify a lessening of the prime minister's reforming zeal. Many of the proposals put forward in the 2005 white paper had, in fact, already been foreshadowed in the Labour Party's election manifesto *Britain Forward Not Back*, where it had been emphasized that education was still the government's "number one priority." A third New

Labour administration would want all secondary schools to become "independent specialist schools, with a strong ethos, high-quality leadership, good discipline (including school uniforms), setting by ability, and high-quality facilities as the norm." There would not be a return to the 11-plus system of the 1950s or "a free-for-all on admissions policies," but it was necessary to ensure that "independent specialist schools tailor education to the needs, interests, and aptitudes of each pupil, within a fair admissions system" (Labour Party, 2005, p. 35).

One of the most controversial proposals in the 2005 white paper was also surrounded by a degree of ambiguity. It would now be open to any existing secondary school—and this would apply to primary schools as well—to create its own trust, or link the school with an existing trust. These trusts would be "not-for- profit" organizations; and could be formed by businesses, charities, faith groups, universities, or parent and community organizations. It was not entirely clear how all this would work out in practice, but it seemed to be the case that self-governing trust schools would have many of the freedoms as those currently enjoyed by the new academies, and be able to appoint the governing body, control their own assets, employ their own staff, and set their own admissions criteria, while "having regard to" the Admissions Code of Practice (DfES, 2005b, p. 25).

The Academies Programme itself would be rapidly expanded: from the 27 open in September 2005, to at least 200 by the end of the decade. Some of the new academies would replace "under-performing" or "failing" schools; others could be entirely new, particularly in London, where there was a demand for new school places resulting from anticipated population growth (DfES, 2005b, p. 29).

As a clear indication of the government's faith in its new projects, it had, in fact, been decided that all new schools would be self-governing foundation schools, trust schools, voluntary-aided schools, or—where appropriate—academies. The schools deemed to be "failing" would be given 12 months in which to improve, and, if such improvement proved unrealizable, a "competition for new providers" would have to be held and the school would be reopened as an academy or as a new trust school, with financial backing provided by a business sponsor or a private charity (DfES, 2005b, pp. 10, 36). It was not envisaged that there would be any circumstances where a new community secondary school would be established.

Both the tone and the agenda of the white paper came in for heavy criticism: from a large number of Labour MPs, from the major teaching unions, and from comprehensive school campaigners. It was feared within the Labour Party that giving certain schools like academies and trust schools greater control over their own admission criteria would have significant implications for the selection of pupils and for the segregation of schools. And there was real anxiety about the clear loss of democratic accountability involved in encouraging private sponsors and faith groups to establish their own educational "brands," grouping schools together in the new ill-defined trusts. It was reported in *The Guardian* (October 26, 2005) that the Dubai-based international education business, GEMS (General Education Management Systems), which already ran 60 low-cost independent schools, was discussing the creation of a "charitable arm," allowing it to enter the new "state schools market." So was the government's agenda really all about the (increased) privatization of the education service (to be discussed more fully in chapter 6)? For Steve Sinnott, the general secretary of the National Union of Teachers, the plans outlined in the white paper were "extraordinarily wrong-headed," where the obsession with choice and private sponsorship ignored the fact that parents already operated on "a far from level playing field." The Blair government was simply "pandering to the pushy middle classes, at the expense of children in less advantaged circumstances" (reported in *The Guardian*, October 25, 2005). And for comprehensive school campaigner Fiona Millar, the idea that certain privileged schools could control their own admissions contradicted the assurance in the party's election manifesto that there would be no "free-for-all on admissions policies," and "no return to 11-plus selection" (Millar, 2005).

Education Secretary Ruth Kelly did not find it easy to answer all these detailed criticisms of the government's policies; and she often appeared uneasy and unsure of herself in media interviews and on public platforms. According to John Dunford, the general secretary of the Association of School and College Leaders (Dunford, 2006, p. 34), she was so taken aback by the strength of the opposition to the idea of much greater autonomy for selected secondary schools that she was often forced to undermine the prime minister's own radical vision for the future of secondary schooling by emphasizing the similarities between proposed trust schools and existing foundation schools. In other words, there was nothing in the white paper that was really new or disruptive. Even so, she experienced a very hostile reception from local government officials and councilors when she tried to defend the government's proposals in a speech to the North of England Education Conference, meeting in Newcastle on January 6, 2006 (reported in *The Guardian*, January 7, 2006).

When the Education and Inspections Bill was published on February 28, 2006, it was obvious that the government had taken note of the white paper's critics in just three key areas. First, there was now to be a stipulation that, when dealing with admissions, all secondary schools would be required to act "in accordance with the Admissions Code," rather than simply "to have regard to it." Second, there was to be a proposed ban on interviewing for selection (other than for boarding places). And, third, local authorities could put forward a new community school, if a new school were needed, or a "failing" school had to be replaced, but only with the approval of the secretary of state. Having granted these fairly minor concessions, the government hoped that future opposition in the House of Commons would be severely weakened.

Yet, there were still fears among opponents of selection and supporters of the comprehensive school, that the future now lay with privately sponsored academies and other "independent state schools," even if the idea of trust schools had to be downplayed and the government chose instead to stress the autonomy of foundation schools. Whatever names were chosen, the secondary school system would clearly become more fragmented and anarchic, with local authorities unable to ensure fairness and justice at a local level. Informal selection could still be practised, and would undoubtedly continue because of the intense competition between secondary schools for the most "able" and "motivated" pupils, leaving the weak and vulnerable to be catered for by schools at the bottom of the popularity charts. Under the legislation, the secretary of state retained a veto over the creation of traditional "community schools"; while there would be no limit to the expansion of faith schools and schools offering a specific specialism.

As it happened, the Education and Inspections Bill passed its second reading in the House of Commons on March 15, 2006—but only with the support of the Conservative opposition. A total of 52 Labour MPs joined the Liberal Democrats in voting against the bill, and 23 Labour MPs abstained. It was thought at one stage that the rebellion could be even larger; but a number of white paper critics were under the illusion that the bill could be further amended at the committee stage. Then, on May 24, 2006, 46 Labour MPs voted against the third reading of the bill, thereby staging the largest House of Commons rebellion ever suffered by a Labour government at third reading.

* * *

Reflections on the Education Initiatives of the Blair Years

New Labour often claimed that it did not want to see a return to the divided secondary system of the 1940s and 1950s; while, at the same time, it rejected the idea of a system made up exclusively of traditional comprehensive schools. We have seen that there were a number of key phrases and slogans that tended to recur in government publications and in speeches by the prime minister and his ministerial team. We were increasingly being told that there was now a need to concentrate on "standards, not structures"; to promote choice and diversity at the secondary level; to reject the idea of the "one-size-fits-all" comprehensive; and to move on to "a post-comprehensive era." To raise educational standards in this changing world, it was necessary to put forward a "third way," even though this was not always clearly articulated, and remained a concept that did not command unanimous support within the Labour Party. It seemed to involve the creation of many new types of secondary school, which would attract the support of the middle and aspirant classes, and thereby help to secure the government's new electoral base. But, for New Labour's critics, this was only half the story; since it could be argued that a rigid hierarchy of schools served chiefly to undermine the Blairite rhetoric of "equality of opportunity," and to sharpen divisions and insecurities.

Chapter 6

The Privatization of Education

Introduction: Different Types of Privatization

One of the dominant themes of at least the past 30 years has been the increasing privatization of significant areas of public provision, including education, and, in this respect, Britain has been pursuing a trend that has a direct parallel in other parts of the world (to be discussed more fully in chapter 8).

According to Professor Stephen Ball, who has made a detailed study of the meaning of privatization where education is concerned, it is important to realize that we are not talking here about a straightforward, one-dimensional phenomenon. The privatization of education is part of a fundamental redesign of the public sector, involving a variety of separate processes; for this reason, it is probably more appropriate to think in terms of "privatizations." In Ball's view, "there is a wide variety of types and forms of privatization, involving different financial arrangements, and different relationships between funders, service providers, and clients" (Ball, 2007, p. 13). What has been described as "a relentless rolling process" (Whitfield, 2001, p. 75) has involved private and "not-for-profit" companies, voluntary and community organizations, and NGOs (nongovernmental organizations) in all manner of income-generating activities within the public sector, especially within health and education.

Professor Richard Pring argued, in a number of academic papers and newspaper articles published in the 1980s (see, for example, Pring,

1983; 1986; 1987a: 1987b), that, in its initial stages, the privatization of education assumed at least two major forms: the purchasing at *private* expense of educational services which ought to have been free within the *public* system; and the purchasing, at *public* expense, of educational services provided by *private*, and often very expensive, institutions. There was possibly a third category, which was privatization in the sense of impoverishing the maintained sector to such an extent that anxious middle-class parents with the necessary means felt more or less obliged to select some form of private schooling for their children. Whatever form it took in the 1980s, the privatization of education could be usefully defined as the systematic erosion, and possibly even abandonment, of the commitment to a common educational service, based on pupil needs rather than upon private means, and accessible to all young people on the basis of equal opportunity. And, as Pring and others have argued, all this was taking place in England against a background of sustained ministerial and media criticism of the performance of the state education system, and as part of the process of subjecting the education service to the same kind of market pressures to which any commercial enterprise would be subjected. Thatcherism clearly involved providing strong ideological and financial support for private education, and also encouraging middle-class "exit" from state institutions.

Pring's first category included the various ways in which parents and community organizations were being asked to pay for both essential and nonessential services within the school at all levels: special lessons or additions to the basic curriculum, resources and books, repairs and maintenance, modifications to the buildings, even teaching posts. It could be argued that there would always be a variety of extracurricular activities—for example, visits to the theatre or school trips, both in this country and abroad—for which parents might well be asked to make an appropriate contribution. But what was happening in the 1980s was that many parents were being expected, not simply to enrich the curriculum *for a few*, but to also facilitate basic curriculum provision *for all*. The National Confederation of Parent Teacher Associations (NCPTA) estimated that, by the middle of the 1980s, £40m a year was being required of parents for what could be regarded as "essentials": books and equipment and lessons (Mountfield, 1991, p. 45). And successive HMI reports pointed to the need for parents to contribute large sums of money, as a means of compensating for a desperate shortage of books and other essential items. This was at a time when Education Secretary Keith Joseph was being widely criticized for his refusal to demand more money for education from the Treasury, with reliance on parental contributions leading to a widening gap between the country's rich and poor schools. The inspectorate noted in their various reports that secondary schools in affluent middle-class areas were in a far better position than were their urban counterparts to find way of compensating for LEA economies, with schools in the shire counties receiving proportionately the greatest levels of additional funding in the form of parental covenants (see Chitty, 1992).

A clear example of Pring's second category was the Assisted Places Scheme, the most radical and controversial of the measures introduced by Margaret Thatcher's first education secretary, Mark Carlisle (1979–1981) (already referred to briefly in the previous chapter). Being a major feature of the 1980 Education Act, and launched in 1981, the scheme was designed to enable "less well-off parents" to claim part or all of the fees at certain independent schools from "a special government fund." It was broadly conceived as a sort of "scholarship ladder," that would benefit "able" children from "poor homes," who would otherwise be "inadequately stretched" at their local "underachieving" comprehensive school. According to Carlisle himself, the chief purpose behind the scheme was "to give certain children a greater opportunity to pursue a particular form of 'academic education', that was regrettably not otherwise, particularly in the cities, available to them" (quoted in Griggs, 1985, p. 89). As far as many Labour critics were concerned, the scheme simply reinforced the view that comprehensive schools were not able to cater to all types of children. Contributing to a heated debate in the House of Lords in September 1982, Labour peer Lord Alexander described the scheme as "an offensive public declaration by a government that the national system of state education is incapable of providing for our most able children" (reported in *The Times Educational Supplement*, September 19, 1982). Subsequent research showed that the scheme did not, in fact, benefit large numbers of those for whom it was supposedly intended, and that it failed to attract a significant number of children from poor or deprived areas of the country (Edwards, Fitz, and Whitty, 1989). As we have already seen, it was abolished by Tony Blair's New Labour government shortly after victory in the 1997 general election.

Early Privatizing Initiatives

The idea of privatizing significant parts of the education service was not part of the education agenda of any of the main political parties in Britain in the 1950s and 1960s, and privatization itself did not occupy a major role in the political discourse of the postwar years. The Institute of Economic Affairs (IEA), which has been described by historian Clive Griggs as the institution which probably deserves the greatest credit for "calling into question the post-war social democratic consensus and moving the political debate to the Right" (Griggs, 1989, p. 101) had indeed been set up as a research and educational trust as early as 1955, and had begun disseminating its right-wing, free-market views in 1957, but its ideas were not really taken seriously within the Conservative Party until the mid-1970s.

As we saw in chapter 3, a significant role in altering the focus of the whole education debate, and in challenging the postwar idea of a "national system, locally administered" was played by the last two black papers, published in 1975 and 1977 (Cox and Boyson, 1975; Cox and Boyson, 1977). In *Black Paper Two*, published in 1969, it had simply been argued that "the need for the times is to extend the possibility of private education to more and more people by making loans and grants available to those who qualify for entrance, but cannot afford the fees" (Cox and Dyson, 1969b, p. 14). In 1975, the editors were urging the introduction of the education voucher in at least two trial areas, as a way of removing responsibility for pupil allocation to secondary schools from local authorities opposed to the idea of parental choice (Cox and Boyson, 1975, p. 4). And the paper even included a special essay by former comprehensive school headteacher Dr. Rhodes Boyson on "The Developing Case for the Educational Voucher' (ibid., pp. 27–28).

Professor Ball has traced the origins of the privatization of education in England back to "the intellectual and political influence of Keith Joseph" (Ball, 2007, p. 17). As we saw in chapter 2, Joseph was instrumental in the development of Margaret Thatcher's political and social philosophy in the 1970s. He had been at the Department of Health and Social Security (DHSS) in Edward Heath's 1970–1974 government, and came to feel a sense of betrayal that an administration committed to letting "lame duck companies" go to the wall, had actually intervened to save both Rolls-Royce Aero Engines and Upper Clyde Shipbuilders. "It was only in 1974 that I was converted to true Conservatism," he wrote in 1975. "I had always thought that I was a Conservative, but now I see that I was not really one at all" (quoted in Young, 1989, p. 79). With Margaret Thatcher and Alfred Sherman, he founded the right-wing think tank—the Centre for Policy Studies—in August 1974; CPS publications were to play a major role in arguing the case for a social market economy, and for the privatization of such important public sector monopolies as education and health. In the view of Joseph and his colleagues, the public sector had, in fact, become a drain on the wealth-creating private sector; and what was needed was more deregulation, liberalization, and privatization. The postwar Keynesian national welfare state had failed; and should be steadily dismantled, replaced by a new emphasis on market-led economic growth and on individual choice and consumption. According to sociologist Anthony Giddens, it was this "antagonism to the Welfare State" that was "one of the most distinctive Neo-liberal traits." He argues that it was seen by Joseph in particular as "the source of all evils," in "much the same way that Capitalism had once been viewed by the Revolutionary Left" (Giddens, 1998a, p.13). It is with good reason that Joseph has been described as "the first Conservative front-bench figure to offer a sustained and broad-ranging challenge to the direction of post-war British economic and social management" (Kavanagh, 1987, p. 115).

When Keith Joseph replaced Mark Carlisle as education secretary in September 1981, it was confidently expected that he would make immediate arrangements for the introduction of the education voucher, as an appropriate means of enhancing parental choice. The scheme had assumed many forms in recent years, but the one that Sir Keith found attractive was based on the simple principle that all parents should be issued with a free basic coupon, that could be "cashed in" at the primary or secondary school of their choice. In a letter he wrote to the Friends of the Education Voucher Experiment in Representative Regions (FEVER) on December 16, 1981, he confirmed that he was "intellectually attracted to the idea of education vouchers as a means of eventually extending parental choice and influence...and of improving educational standards" (reprinted in Seldon, 1986, p. 36). Yet this was one occasion when he was unable to proceed without the support of his civil servants, who were only too aware of all the practical and political difficulties involved in introducing a voucher experiment, on a local or a national basis, particularly since the proposed scheme could do very little to solve the problem of intense competition for places at the most popular schools. In a written statement to the House of Commons in June 1984, the education secretary was forced to concede that the voucher scheme, at least in the foreseeable future, was dead:

> I was intellectually attracted to the idea of education vouchers, because they seemed to offer the possibility of some kind of market mechanism, which would increase the choice and diversity of schools in response to the wishes of parents acting as consumers. But in the course of my examination of this possibility, it became clear that there would be great practical difficulties in making any voucher system compatible with the requirements that schooling should be available to all, without charge, compulsory, and of an acceptable standard.... These requirements... were seen to limit substantially the operation, and the benefits, of free-market choices; and to entail an involvement on the part of the State—centrally and locally—which would be both financial and regulatory, and on a scale likely to necessitate an administrative effort as great as under the present system. These factors would have applied, whether vouchers were to become available only within the maintained system, or could be used in the independent sector as well.
>
> A change of this magnitude would desirably be preceded by pilot schemes undertaken by volunteer LEAs. These would require legislation, and there was serious doubt as to whether they could adequately establish the feasibility of a voucher scheme within a manageable time scale.
>
> I concluded that the difficulties which would arise from the many and complex changes required to the legal and institutional framework of the education system, and the additional cost of mitigating them, were too great to justify further consideration of a voucher system, as a means of increasing parental choice and influence....
>
> For these reasons, the idea of vouchers is no longer on the agenda. (*Hansard*, H. of C., Sixth Series—Vol. 62, col. 290, written answers to questions, June 22, 1984)

At the time, the abandonment of the education voucher (temporary or otherwise) was seen by many as a victory for the conservative forces at the heart of the political establishment. For example, an editorial which appeared in *The Daily Telegraph* on January 13, 1986 argued that

> measures dear to the Prime Minister's heart which have fallen by the wayside include education vouchers and student loans.... Though her aspirations reflect popular feeling, they run counter to those of the political classes, the establishment, by now accustomed to rule, whomever *demos* elects.

And this view was echoed by Arthur Seldon, formerly editorial director of the Institute of Economic Affairs, who argued in an IEA Hobart paperback that the reason for Sir Keith's decision was "not administrative impracticability, but official feet-dragging and political underestimation of potential popular acclaim (and the votes that would accrue) (Seldon, 1986, p. 97).

The one major privatizing initiative that *did* get off the ground during Margaret Thatcher's period as prime minister was the City Technology College (CTC) Project announced by Keith Joseph's successor, Kenneth Baker, at the 1986 Conservative Party conference, and which was to serve as a prototype for New Labour's City Academies Programme. Reference has already been made to this project in previous chapters, and it was significant in many ways, but its importance, as far as the theme of *this* chapter is concerned, lies in its innovative approach to the funding of schools.

It was confidently expected by Baker and his advisers that the new colleges, which would be independent of local authority control, would be financed to a very large extent by private capital, and that the response from wealthy industrialists would be so great that 20 new colleges would be up and running by the beginning of the 1990s. The original idea was, in fact, that between £8 and £10 million would be put up by wealthy backers toward capital costs, with the government's contribution being relatively minimal. As it happened, majority of the large firms boycotted the CTC Scheme, anxious, in many cases, not to damage their good relations with existing secondary schools under local authority control; so widespread was the feeling of caution and doubt that of the 1,800 major enterprises initially approached, only 17 responded positively (Chitty, 1989b, p. 40). Even where money was forthcoming, it was *never* in the quantities Kenneth Baker hoped for. For example, in the case of the Djanogly CTC in Nottingham, which eventually opened in September 1989, the government was forced to donate £9.05 million from the Treasury to augment the £1.4 million subscribed by private companies—leading an editorial in *The Times Educational Supplement* to comment with uncharacteristic bitterness on May 27, 1988:

> Just what sort of a public education initiative is it which puts up £9 million from public funds for what is, in effect, a private school? And just what sort of priorities are being pursued when one, as yet unbuilt, private school gets £9.05 million, while the county of Nottinghamshire's entire capital allocation is less than £2.5 million?

The government spent £33 million on the first three CTCs established in 1988 and 1989—some £3 million more than had been set aside for the introduction of the National Curriculum into all 30,000 schools in the country. From the outset, it was clear that the amount of private capital given or pledged to the CTC project would be out-matched by the enormous amount of public money committed to the scheme, and this disparity led Shadow Education Secretary Jack Straw to complain in a House of Commons debate at the end of June 1988 that "the Government's original intention of setting up public schools with private money has now changed to setting up private schools with public money" (quoted in *Education*, July 8, 1988).

Kenneth Baker finally decided that the government would have to be satisfied with £2 million or less as sponsorship money for each new CTC, and, coincidentally, as we shall see later in this chapter, this was the figure that New Labour (learning from the Conservatives' obvious mistakes) decided on for each of its own new City Academies, established after 2000. Where CTCs were concerned, the college that opened at Kingswood in Bristol in September 1993 turned out to be the last such college to be authorized.

Conservative support for privatization in general, and for the privatization of education in particular, was certainly growing in momentum in the second half of the 1980s. In a profile of Oliver Letwin, published in *The Independent* in June 1988, the former special adviser to Keith Joseph was quoted as saying that

> Nationalized enterprises always drag officials and ministers into opposing the customers' interests. Once privatization is complete in this country, the role of ministers in running everything will never be

restored.... Britain is now moving into a position where people in government do not think it is their business to run anything. Four hundred years from now, people will still be talking about Mrs. Thatcher. And it will be because of that profound shift in the way government thinks. (Quoted in Hughes, 1988)

Another of Joseph's key advisers, and a founding member of the Centre for Policy Studies, Sir Alfred Sherman, argued in an interview with *The Daily Telegraph*, on August 6, 1987, that in so many of its aspects, the Thatcherite revolution was simply brilliant; but that it would be incomplete, "without the privatization of all schools." Further progress in the "liberalization" and privatization of society was also advocated by Sir Geoffrey Howe, Mrs. Thatcher's then foreign secretary, in a wide-ranging speech to a meeting of Conservatives in the City of London at the beginning of June 1988

> The new frontier of Conservatism—or, rather, the later stage in that rolling frontier—is about reforming those parts of the state sector, which the privatizing process has so far left largely untouched: those activities in our society, such as health and education, which together consume a third of our national income, but where market opportunities are still hardly known. (Quoted in *The Independent,* June 7, 1988)

And a delegate to a Young Conservative conference held in Southport in February 1989 received rapturous applause, when he told his audience that it was time both to "proclaim education a commodity to be bought and sold," and to "disclaim the Marxist view that education is a human right" (quoted in *The Guardian*, February 13, 1989).

The privatization of education might seem a fairly straightforward and unproblematic process, but the type of private company or business deemed "suitable" for sponsoring a secondary school was often the subject of media scrutiny in the 1990s; this was especially the case when it was announced by the Education Secretary Gillian Shephard in May 1996, that the tobacco giant BAT Industries had agreed to provide at least £100,000 sponsorship for one of the Major government's new technology specialist schools. (A previous Conservative government had already attracted criticism for allowing BAT to donate more than £2 million to the Macmillan City Technology College in Middlesbrough, set up in September 1989). The decision to welcome BAT Industries as an appropriate sponsor for a second time was described in an editorial in *The Times Educational Supplement* (May 24, 1996), as "a gift for the political satirists"; since this was also a time when the government was spending millions of pounds in an attempt to discourage teenagers from taking up smoking.

It was also in the 1990s that the government of John Major effectively "privatized" the inspection process for state schools. The Education (Schools) Act of 1992, to which reference was made in the last chapter, established Ofsted (Office for Standards in Education) as a new "independent" body, responsible for contracting independent teams to inspect all state primary and secondary schools. The number of HMIs (Her Majesty's Inspectors) was to be greatly reduced, from nearly 500 to 175; and the relationship between the schools and the inspectorate was to be radically transformed, since many headteachers found it impossible to view the new Ofsted inspectors as allies in the process of improving schools.

New Labour's Approach to Privatization

How, then, did New Labour under Tony Blair respond to the liberalizing and privatizing agenda of the Thatcher and Major administrations, especially with regard to all aspects of social policy?

In a 1998 pamphlet for the right-wing Institute of Economic Affairs (IEA), a think tank which acquired prominence during the Thatcher years, Michael Novak proudly asserted that "the triumph of Tony Blair may...be regarded as the triumph of Margaret Thatcher" (Novak, 1998, p. 2). This would appear to support the view of policy analysts Sally Power and Geoff Whitty that at least as far as New Labour's education program was concerned, Blair's policy agenda could be said to "follow the path of the New Right, rather than pick up the threads of the Old Left" (Power and Whitty, 1999, p. 543). Yet, in putting forward his own ideas for the creation of a "middle" or "third" way between Thatcherism and Socialism, Professor Anthony Giddens specifically rejected the widely held criticism of the Third Way approach, or at least Blair's version of it, as simply "warmed-over Neo-liberalism" (Giddens, 1998a, p. 25); and, in a spirited critique of Novak's thesis, also argued that the triumph of New Labour in the 1990s actually confirmed "the failure, and not the success, of Thatcherism and Neo-liberalism in a general sense" (Giddens, 1998b, p. 27).

While the precise positioning of Blair's political philosophy is open to debate, it would appear to be widely accepted that there were both significant *continuities* and significant *ruptures* between Thatcherism and Blairism. As defined by Stephen Ball (2007) and Andrew Gamble (1988), Thatcherism involved a number of crucial factors: freeing the market, shrinking the state, and reducing civil society to little more than the competing interests of "consumer-citizens." Blair's post-neo-Liberal "Third Way" retained many of the key privatizing elements of Thatcherism, but retained a role for the state in managing capitalism, and in dealing with some of the more glaring inequalities created by "free-market" relationships.

It is certainly true that for New Labour ministers, privatization rapidly came to be seen as a more or less permanent feature of the social and political scene. During his first and second administrations, Tony Blair used a number of important speeches to make clear his determination to use *private sector* practice to push through *public sector* reform. This was to be his basic message, taken from a speech on public service reform, delivered in October 2001:

> In developing greater choice of provider, the private and voluntary sectors can play an important role. Contrary to myth, no one has ever suggested that they are *the* answer. Or that they should actually *replace* public services. But where use of them can improve our public services, nothing should stand in the way of their use. In any event, round the world, the barriers between public, private and voluntary are coming down.... If schools want a new relationship with business in their community, as many do, let them have it.... What I'm saying is: let the system breathe; develop; expand; let the innovation and creative ideas of the private sector be given a chance to flourish. (Prime minister's speech on public service reform, October 16, 2001, quoted in Ball, 2007, p. 36)

An early example of a New Labour privatizing initiative in education could be said to be the short-lived Education Action Zones Project, announced, as we have seen, in the 1997 white paper *Excellence in Schools*, and actually launched in 1998. The first 25 Zones (12 starting in September 1998, and 13 in January 1999) were selected on the basis of competitive bids and would operate for just three years in the first instance. It was intended that they would be a bold new venture, "uniting private companies, schools, local education authorities, and parents"—in the cause of "modernizing education in areas of social deprivation" (DfEE, 1998, p. 2). They were an important indication of what was to come, although they were soon to be subsumed within the government's Excellence in Cities Programme.

In 1998, Surrey County Council invited companies to bid for the contract to run one of its comprehensive schools, King's Manor in Guildford, deemed to be "failing." And in February 1999, it was announced that the contract had been won by 3Es Enterprises Ltd, a private company set up as the commercial arm of Kingshurst City Technology College, which had opened in the West Midlands borough of Solihull in 1988. The managing director of 3Es was, in fact, the husband of the first principal of the Kingshurst CTC.

Then it was announced in November 1999 that Cambridge Education Associates—a consultancy that was also the largest contractor for school inspections—was the preferred bidder to assume responsibility for all (or nearly all) the functions of Islington Local Education Authority in north London, making this the first major privatization of an LEA. Hackney Local Education Authority was already in the process of having *some* of its education services privatized; but Islington was the first to have *all* its education services taken over by a private limited company. When announcing the government's decision to the media, the then schools minister Estelle Morris said that Islington and the DfEE were determined that this would mark "a new beginning." She went on to say that she hoped services would be privatized in a similar fashion "in up to 15 more local education authorities." It was her view that privatization was "the obvious solution" to the long-standing problems that many local education authorities faced (reported in *The Independent*, November 27, 1999).

Private Finance Initiative

As we saw in the previous section, in the early years of the Blair administration, private enterprise was able to play a significant role in education initiatives, both in the sponsorship of projects designed to provide new and challenging opportunities for youngsters in "tough inner-city areas," and in the running of so-called failing institutions. It had become obvious, in the course of the 1990s, that many of the markets for "traditional" consumer goods were reaching saturation point, so the expanding markets of the future would be in essential services such as health and education. Many private firms were now anxious to be given the chance to run public services, in return for a more or less guaranteed stream of income from the state.

The clearest example of how private capital could make such a low-risk investment with guaranteed returns was the Private Finance Initiative (PFI), a scheme that had been launched in the early 1990s, and which constituted in many respects the most radical and far-reaching of the privatizing initiatives of the last two decades. Indeed, its repercussions are still being felt under the coalition government of today. From the outset, it involved the use of private sector funding to provide new buildings and facilitate major refurbishments across the public sector. In essence, it meant the injection of private capital into a wide range of public services, especially education, health, and transport, in return for lucrative long-term service contracts and the heady prospect, for the private company or group of private companies concerned, of being able to benefit from a long period of financial stability and steady growth. In the majority of cases, PFI contracts, involving new buildings and facilities management, were designed to last for between 25 and 35 years, and, once negotiated, they were almost impossible to dismantle. During that period, the private sector company or companies providing the capital could expect to be more than adequately reimbursed by the relevant public agency—invariably a health trust or a local education authority. In the case of schools, the private company or consortium responsible for the initial construction of the new building could also expect to assume responsibility for the management and maintenance of the premises, and this would include responsibility for such important aspects of facilities management as essential repairs, grounds maintenance, cleaning, catering, oversight of all utilities, and the provision of items of furniture and IT equipment.

PFI was not a New Labour initiative: it had, in fact, been launched by John Major's government in late 1992. Nevertheless, its use was intensified after Blair's electoral victory in 1997; and PFI projects came to form part of PPPs (Public Private Partnerships), embracing a wide range of possible contractual and collaborative relationships between public authorities and private sector companies. Such projects proved attractive to governments, in that they appeared to reduce public borrowing requirements. They also had the effect of reducing capital spending—or at least postponing it to future years. At the same time, they were attractive to local authorities, in so far as they provided funding for capital building projects, which might not have been forthcoming otherwise. It was claimed on behalf of PFI and PPP projects, that they both provided "value for money" *and* invariably delivered "efficient services." More cynical users of PFI might have had reservations about such claims; but they had to concede that there really was no alternative source of income. At a conference held in 2000, the finance directors of Birmingham and Glasgow local authorities, both major users of PFI, cast doubts on the "value-for-money" claims being made for the schemes. George Black, the finance director for Glasgow, said: "I'm not sure it *is* value for money. But it's the only game in town. It is the only way you get money back into your services" (quoted in Ball, 2007, p. 47).

Not surprisingly, PFI schemes proved enormously attractive to the construction industry, and afforded the prospect of considerable growth. For example: the Major Contractors Group (MCG), which lobbied governments on behalf of the industry, was prepared to concede, in 2004, that companies involved in PFI work, building schools and hospitals, could "expect to make between three and ten times as much money as was possible on more traditional contracts." In expanding on this point, Bill Tallis, the managing director of MCG, admitted that "construction firms traditionally received rates of return of 1.5 percent to 2 percent on normal contracts, but were now expecting margins of 7.5 percent to 15 percent on PFI building schemes (*Corporate Watch*, March 19, 2004, quoted in Ball, 2007, p. 46).

It was for this sort of reason that PFI schemes often attracted criticism. It seemed to be the case that such schemes were often more expensive than were more traditional publicly funded projects of a similar nature; and that, in general, it cost local education authorities more to negotiate with private contractors than to make use of loans from the government. On top of the normal costs, there were the fees for consultants and the profit taken by the PFI companies themselves. It was calculated by Richard Hatcher, in 2001, that PFI building projects cost at least 10 percent more than schemes financed in more traditional ways; Hatcher went on to highlight some of the implications of using this method of funding to secure new or refurbished buildings. "Firms could receive government approval only if they could demonstrate 'value for money,' and this meant they had to reduce costs by operating schools more 'efficiently,' on facilities management contracts which employed fewer staff and made greater use of flexible contracts, and which sought to increase income generation through the charges for the private and community use of school premises" (Hatcher, 2001, p. 67).

The first two schools to be financed by PFI contracts were opened in 1999, and the Labour government's building program (Building Schools for the Future) was expected to make use of PFI funding. By the beginning of 2005, there were 86 PFI school projects in England, worth £2.4 billion, involving over five hundred schools, 15 in Scotland worth £553 million, and just two in Wales. The overall value of PFI schemes at that time was estimated by the Treasury to be £7.7 billion, including £900 million for educational and skills projects. In the beginning, sponsors of the government's new (City) Academies were reluctant to make use of PFI funding, preferring to keep a tight control over the building and day-to-day management of their schools.

Assessing the overall significance of private-public partnerships, Stephen Ball argued that "the multi-faceted nature of PFIs reworks the landscape of public sector provision, and is a crucial part of the repositioning of local government as service commissioners" (Ball, 2007, pp. 47–48). And, from the outset, the government itself was also quite frank in acknowledging that PFI or PPP was not just about the funding of capital projects; it entailed a radical redefinition of provision in the public services, with most local authorities now forced to accept a marked reduction in their service provision role:

> PFI or PPP is one of the Government's main instruments for delivering higher quality and more cost-effective public services, with the public sector as an *enabler*, and, where appropriate, guardian of the interests of the users and customers of the public services. It is not simply about the financing of capital investment in services; but about exploiting the full range of private sector management, commercial and creative skills. (Press Release, Lord Chancellor's Department, February 8, 1998)

As we shall explore more fully in chapter 8, there has also been a global dimension to private capital's colonization of the public sector, with Britain being far from alone in envisaging a much reduced role for the state. The global mechanism for opening up large areas of state education to the private sector was the General Agreement on Trade and

Services (GATS), which was part of the agenda at the Seattle round of the World Trade Organization in 1999. And the World Bank was keen to observe in the same year that "although the State still has a central role in ensuring the provision of basic services—education, health, infrastructure—it is not obvious that the State must be the *only* provider, or, indeed, a provider at all" (quoted in Hatcher, 2001, p. 63).

The Academies Programme

As we have already noted, the educational and political principles underpinning New Labour's Academies Programme owed a great deal to the rationale behind Kenneth Baker's City Technology Colleges Project. And it is surely significant that the statutory basis for the new academies was the collection of legislative powers taken from the 1988 Education Reform Act, and originally intended to facilitate the establishment of a nationwide network of CTCs. All that was necessary was a last-minute amendment to the 2000 Education and Skills Bill, which was not, in fact introduced until June 27, 2000, after the bill had passed through the House of Lords, and towards the very end of the Commons Committee stage—a highly unusual procedure for a major initiative of this kind.

The Academies Programme had actually been launched by Education Secretary David Blunkett, in a speech delivered to the Social Market Foundation (SMF) on March 15, 2000, where he announced that the government's program had been conceived as "a radical approach" to "breaking the cycle of underperformance and low expectations" in inner-city schools. This was at the core of his vision for the new academies outlined in the speech (and in an accompanying press release and booklet):

> These Academies, to replace "seriously failing schools," will be built and managed by partnerships involving the Government, voluntary, church, and business sponsors. They will offer a real challenge and improvements in pupil performance, for example through innovative approaches to management. governance, teaching and the curriculum, including a specialist focus in at least one curriculum area.... They will also be committed to working with and learning from other local

schools.... The aim will be to raise standards by breaking the cycle of underperformance and low expectations. To be eligible for government support, the Academies will all need to meet clear criteria. They will take over or replace existing schools, which are either in special measures, or underachieving. (http:/www.dfes.gov.uk/speeches; see also Rogers and Migniulo, 2007, p. 7)

The education department's accompanying press notice said: "The new approach of the Academies Programme will bring a radical new edge to the Government's Fresh Start Initiative—strengthening our policies, designed to turn failure into school improvement" (DfES press release, March 15, 2000).

The first three City Academies opened in September 2002. Nine followed a year later, and five more opened in September 2004, making a total of 17 during Tony Blair's second term in office. (It is important to note that at an early stage in the development of the program, the word "City" was dropped—to allow for the future creation of new schools in *rural* areas). The *Five Year Strategy for Children and Learners*, published in July 2004, predicted that the government would have at least 200 academies "open or in the pipeline" by the year 2010, irrespective of the fact that no assessment would have been made of either their academic achievements or their cost-effectiveness. According to the *Strategy*, some would replace "under-performing schools"; while others could be entirely new, particularly in London, where there was a clear demand for new school places, and where it was anticipated that there would be 60 new academies by 2010 (DfES, 2004a, pp. 9, 51). As we have already seen, Labour ministers were determined not to repeat the Conservatives' mistakes where initial funding was concerned; and decided on £2 million as the appropriate figure to be asked of the sponsor or joint sponsors for each new academy. However, even this modest sum had to be abandoned later, where sponsors such as universities and private schools were concerned.

Many of New Labour's academies proved very popular with parents and were soon massively oversubscribed; but, for left-wing critics, there were worrying issues related to sponsorship and accountability. A front-page story with the title: "Should These People Be Running State Schools?" that appeared in *The Independent* on July 8, 2004, written by the newspaper's education editor Richard Garner, pointed out that by the end of that decade, the "secondary education landscape in England" would have been "transformed," with "a whole swathe of state-maintained schools throughout the country handed over to private sponsors to run." The people in charge of our schools would be "the bankers, various church leaders, the millionaire philanthropists, and the leaders of the country's private schools"—all in the name of "providing more choice for parents and raising school standards" (Garner, 2004).

One of the key individuals named in Richard Garner's article was Sir Peter Vardy, the millionaire car dealer who had just acquired control of King's Academy in Middlesbrough, opened in September 2003, and whose first school, Emmanuel City Technology College in Gateshead, opened in September 1990, gave its name to the foundation that Sir Peter's car dealer firm, Reg Vardy plc, financed. Sir Peter was, in fact, the first person to come forward with an offer to sponsor one or more City Academies soon after David Blunkett made his initial announcement; and he rapidly earned the admiration and respect of Tony Blair. The main reason for all the controversy surrounding Sir Peter's activities, highlighted by Richard Garner in his *Independent* article, lay in the fact that he was a committed and outspoken creationist believing that the Bible was telling the literal truth when it revealed that the universe was created by God in six days, and that this event took place in 4004 BC (see Beckett, 2007, p. 72). It followed that this biblical truth *must* underpin the curriculum in any school or college run by the Emmanuel Foundation. According to a document entitled *Christianity and Curriculum*, which Sir Peter had arranged to be available on the website of Emmanuel College, science teachers at the school were expected to teach creationism alongside evolution, and history teachers were required to understand the importance of using "a frame of reference in which God is sovereign," stressing that there could well be occasions in world history, such as at the time of Hitler's planned invasion of Britain in the Summer of 1940, when God intervened to ensure that "good triumphed" and "the march of Evil was halted" (reported in *The Times*, July 24, 2002). Liberal Democrats, senior church figures, and a group of prominent scientists called for an urgent government inquiry, when it was reported in *The Guardian*, in March 2002, that Emmanuel College had hosted a "creationist conference," and that Sir Peter had said at this event that all his teachers were expected to promote something called "Biblical Fundamentalism" (*The Guardian*, March 9, 2002). Questioned in the House of Commons about the use of taxpayers' money to fund the teaching of creationism at Emmanuel College, Prime Minister Tony Blair neatly sidestepped the question, by saying:

> I think it would be very unfortunate if concerns over this issue were seen to remove the very, very strong incentive to make sure we get as diverse a school system as we possibly can.... In the end, it is a more diverse school system that will deliver better results for our children, and if you look at the actual results of this College, I think you will find that they are very good. (Reported in *The Guardian*, March 14, 2002)

When Nigel McQuoid became head of King's Academy in 2003, he said the criticism of creationism was totally misplaced, and that schools should teach the creation story, as literally depicted in *Genesis* (reported in *The Guardian*, January 15, 2005).

Despite the criticisms and reservations relating to individual sponsors, the number of academies grew rapidly in the 13-year period of the Blair and Brown administrations. As we have already seen, there were already 17 academies in existence by the beginning of 2005. A further 10 opened in September 2005 and 19 in September 2006, bringing the total to 46. In a speech at a Specialist Schools and Academies Trust conference in November 2006, Tony Blair announced a doubling of the 2005 target figure to 400—but with no specific reference to the anticipated timescale (reported in *The Guardian*, November 19, 2006). It was also at this event that he predicted that some of the new schools would be aimed at catering to pupils aged 3–19.

When New Labour eventually left office in May, 2010, the number of academies bequeathed to the Conservative-led coalition government was, in fact, just 203; but it was already clear by then that the program would enjoy the Conservatives' unqualified support. Indeed, speaking to a conference of the CBI (Confederation of British Industry) in May 2007, the then shadow education secretary, David Willetts, announced that a Conservative government would be "happy to adopt Tony Blair's Academies," which were, in any case, a "diluted version" of the Conservatives' City Technology Colleges Project. There would be no requirement for outside sponsors to contribute £2 million, and there would be an insistence on the adoption of whole-class teaching and setting by ability. At the same time, there would be no commitment to the establishment of any new grammar schools, since it had to be conceded that these selective schools had only 2 percent of pupils on free school meals, and it was Tony Blair's academies that offered the genuine prospect of unlimited social mobility (reported in *The Guardian*, May 17, 2007).

Before leaving office, and mindful of the criticism that New Labour had been far too anxious to attract wealthy entrepreneurs, with no academic credentials, as academy sponsors, ministers made speeches designed to legitimize the Academies Project. In his last Mansion House speech as chancellor of the exchequer before taking over from Tony Blair as prime minister, Gordon Brown announced that the expansion of the Academies Programme would be one of the "clear priorities" of his forthcoming administration, and that he was determined that higher education should be encouraged to play "a fuller part in the sponsorship of the new schools" (reported in *The Guardian*, June 21, 2007). To win over the support of leading universities, it had been decided that they should be allowed to sponsor new academies at a discounted rate.

In a speech at the Headmasters' and Headmistresses' Conference (HMC), delivered on October 2, 2007, Schools Minister Lord Adonis, very much the chief architect of the Academies Project since 2000, announced that, as with the universities, any independent school wishing to sponsor an academy would *not* be required to contribute £2 million toward the starting costs. In an interview with Polly Curtis, education editor of *The Guardian*, ahead of the speech, Lord Adonis said:

> Successful independent schools will henceforth be exempt from the £2 million sponsorship requirement when they set up or support an Academy. It is their educational DNA we are seeking, not their fee income, or their existing charitable endowments. (*The Guardian*, October 2, 2007)

The speech was made in the face of opposition from fee-paying parents, who objected to any of their money being spent on outside state schools sponsored by the private sector.

It was very much a feature of New Labour's final years in office that the more successful independent schools were encouraged to sponsor academies, partner so-called failing state schools, and help failing private schools to opt for academy status (see Benn, 2011, p. 151). Dulwich College in south-east London took on the Isle of Sheppey Academy;

The Skinners' School sponsored The Skinners' Kent Academy, both schools being located in Tunbridge Wells; and Wellington College, run by Anthony Seldon, sponsored the Wellington Academy in Wiltshire, opened in September 2009. Of the other independent schools, 12 opted to become cosponsors; and 13 chose to become "educational partners." The United Learning Trust, whose sister charity, the United Church Schools Trust, already ran ten fee-charging schools, recruited two educational cosponsors from the independent sector, Marlborough College and Winchester College, for two of its 17 academies. A letter drawn up by two of the leading independent school heads Anthony Seldon and Graham Able, the then master of Dulwich College, and signed by eight colleagues for publication in April 2008, drew attention to the reasons why the private sector should be involved in the running of state schools:

> In our case, "sponsorship" involves academic and administrative leadership and governance.... We do not think we have *all* the answers, but we do feel that the success within our sector suggests that we have something to offer in helping the establishment and development of the new Academies. (Quoted in Garner, 2008).)

* * *

New Labour's Stance on Privatization and the Emerging Educational Scene

In an article for *The Financial Times*, published on March 10, 2008, Prime Minister Gordon Brown argued that it was now time for New Labour to implement "the third act in public sector reform," which would involve the privatization and revitalization of the education service. According to Brown's analysis of the government's long-term public sector reform program—and particularly in relation to education and health—the *first* act, indeed New Labour's *first* task in 1997, had demanded "a programme of investment and repair, designed to remedy decades of neglect under the Conservatives, and to establish a basic level of standards, below which no school or hospital would fall." This had inevitably meant using national targets, league tables, and tough inspection regimes to monitor progress. To ensure that the government obtained "maximum value from each pound spent," and that "struggling services were turned round," the *second* state of the reform program had focused on "tackling under-performance, and on reducing variations in standards." It was now time to go further, and move on to the *third* act—the *third* stage of reform where, in the case of education, choice and diversity were enhanced, and new private providers were brought in to "create the dynamism for transforming under-performing secondary schools." The government's strategy was to "empower and enable more of our best headteachers to help turn round low-performing schools, to create new 'trusts' and federations around successful schools, and, in areas of greatest need, to drive forward an even faster expansion of the Government's Academies Programme." There could be "no backtracking on reform, no go-slow, no reversals, and no easy compromises" (Brown, 2008).

Largely as a result of New Labour education policy, pursued with great vigor since 2000, the privatization of schools is a development that has come to dominate the educational landscape; and it has been argued (Benn, 2011, p. 121) that "possibly the biggest trend in this new 'edu-market' is the growth of 'chains'—organizations running large groups of schools, often nationwide, with sufficient resources to rival those of a local authority." Of these many organizations, the most influential have turned out to be: the Academies Enterprise Trust; ARK (Absolute Return for Kids); Cambridge Education Associates, whose UK portfolio includes the running of all education services for the London Borough of Islington; the Capita Group; CfBT; the Cognita Group, founded in 2004 by former chief inspector of schools Chris Woodhead, and currently the largest private operator of schools in the UK; E-ACT (Edutrust Academies Charitable Trust); GEMS (Global Education Management Systems); the Harris Federation; the Oasis Trust; the Priory Federation; and ULT (the United Learning Trust). To quote from the ATL (Association of Teachers and Lecturers) publication *England's Schools: Not Open for Business*, dating from September 2010, this radically expanding role for private enterprise has meant the undermining of "a basic principle of the 1944 Education Act" that schools should remain "a public service under direct local democratic control, administered by people who know the schools, the local area, and the local people" (ATL, 2010, p. 3).

Chapter 7

The Erosion of the National Curriculum

Introduction

As we noted briefly in chapter 2, it was Margaret Thatcher's truncated third administration (1987–1990) that saw the introduction of a national curriculum for all state primary and secondary schools in England and Wales. But it is often forgotten that the decision by Education Secretary Kenneth Baker (1986–1989), with the support of his senior civil servants, to include far-reaching curriculum proposals as part of the 1987 Education Bill did not have the wholehearted support of Conservative MPs at Westminster, nor indeed of the Conservative cabinet. The very idea of a centrally determined state curriculum was the subject of bitter dispute among the various sections of the so-called New Right, and there were many influential thinkers advising the prime minister who argued that a rigid program of study could have no place in a market system of schools, where a school's unique curriculum framework could well be one of its essential "selling-points."

Mrs. Thatcher herself was one of those who felt that anything more ambitious than a strictly limited "core" curriculum of "compulsory" subjects was actually at variance with the Right's program for creating more choice and variety in the system, particularly at the secondary level, and she made her views known on a number of occasions. The National Curriculum Consultation Document listing the foundation subjects to be taken by all pupils during their compulsory education was published in July 1987 (DES, 1987); and it seems that debates in cabinet in the Summer and Autumn of 1997 focused on the actual amount of time that a ten-subject curriculum would take up in a typical secondary school in a 40-period week.

In his 1993 autobiography *The Turbulent Years: My Life in Politics*, Kenneth Baker revealed, in a passage of remarkable candor, that as late as October 1987—just *three* weeks before the introduction of the Education Reform Bill into the House of Commons—he had felt obliged to use the threat of his own resignation to prevent his broad-based curriculum being radically amended by Margaret Thatcher:

> I saw the Prime Minister privately. And I said to her: "If you want me to continue as your Education Secretary, then we will have to stick to the Curriculum that I set out in the July 1987 Consultation Paper. I and my ministerial colleagues have advocated and stoutly defended our broad-based curriculum. We have listed the ten subjects, and I set them out before the Select Committee in April. You will recall, Prime Minister, that I had specifically cleared my statement with you."...I reminded her that the Education Reform Bill was going to be introduced in three weeks' time, and that the curriculum part of it had already been drafted. All our Parliamentary draftsmen were working flat out drawing up the rest. It was simply the case that I couldn't change the clauses dealing with the Curriculum at this late stage even if I had wanted to, and I didn't.... This was a tough meeting; but I was simply not prepared to give in to a last-minute rearguard action, even when waged by the Prime Minister herself. The broad-based Curriculum was saved—for the time being. (Baker, 1993, p. 197)

Kenneth Baker got his way on this occasion; but Mrs. Thatcher and many of her more extreme advisers continued to feel that the Conservatives were responsible for a bill that lacked consistency and was ideologically flawed

In the event, Section Three of the 1988 Act, based on the 1987 Bill, listed the "core" and "foundation" subjects that were to constitute the new National Curriculum for England and Wales:

The "core" subjects were to be:

(a) mathematics, English, and science; and
(b) in relation to schools in Wales that were Welsh-speaking schools, Welsh.

The "foundation" subjects were to be:

(a) history, geography, technology, music, art, and physical education; and
(b) in relation to the third and fourth key stages, a modern foreign language; and
(c) in relation to schools in Wales that were *not* Welsh-speaking schools, Welsh.

A further subject, religious education (the only subject that was actually compulsory in the period from 1944 to 1988, but somehow overlooked in the rush to get the 1987 consultation paper published) was to continue to be a compulsory subject for all state pupils—as the one and only *basic* subject. It was anticipated that the majority of curriculum time at the primary stage in England would be taken up with work in the three "core" subjects: mathematics, English and science. And this was to be very much a subject-based curriculum with new themes, such as health education and information technology, to be taught through the relevant "foundation" subjects at Key Stages Three and Four.

In the view of Stuart Sexton, one of the prime minister's principal advisers on education, and director of the education unit of the Institute of Economic Affairs (IEA), this section of the 1988 act represented an attempt by the education secretary to impose a "nationalized curriculum" on the country, and signified a betrayal of all the principles that the Conservative Party ought to uphold. While the Education Bill was still making its way through parliament, he had written an article for *The Times*, warning of the dangers lurking in Kenneth Baker's reforms:

> The Government's curriculum proposals will put the school curriculum into a straitjacket, removing all flexibility, and retarding the continual process of improvement and updating. Once these proposals are put into tablets of legislative stone, it will be years before the bureaucracy wakes up, both to its own mistakes, and to the need to make necessary changes. (Sexton, 1988)

And, interviewed in November 1995, Sexton argued that the curriculum proposals in the 1988 act constituted a quite *separate* and *unnecessary* piece of legislation, serving merely to divert attention away from the laudable free-market objectives that most members of the prime minister's Policy Unit had been working toward:

> Well, in my view, that Great Education Reform Act was really *two* Acts of Parliament. Now, one of those Acts of Parliament was the one that the Policy Unit and I had been working on in the latter days of Keith Joseph,... for the better management and financing of our schools, and there you will find CTCs and Grant-Maintained Schools, and all the rest of it. That was the Education Bill we cared about. The second Act of Parliament...which got pushed in at the last minute, was all to do with this central control over the school curriculum, and I can claim no credit for that, and neither do all the others who were working with me under Keith in the early 1980s. There was this constant wish of so many civil servants at the DES going back years and years to take control of the school curriculum, although even they didn't expect the new National Curriculum and the various syllabuses to be quite so detailed and prescriptive as they turned out to be. And it all went through in spite of the opposition of Mrs. Thatcher's chief political advisers. (Sexton, 1995)

In April 1990, Mrs. Thatcher herself surprised both ministers and DES civil servants by arguing, in an interview with the editor of *The Sunday Telegraph*, that the National Curriculum was becoming far too prescriptive. She pointed out that she had never intended that the National *Curriculum* should become a sort of national *syllabus*, and she drew a sharp distinction between the "core" subjects of the original framework and the seven other "foundation" subjects:

> The core curriculum—and by that I mean proposals for the English, the mathematics and the science—now that was what I always meant by a *national* curriculum. Everyone simply *must* be trained in mathematics, up to a certain standard. You *must* be trained in language, and I would also say some literature, up to a certain standard. You really *must*. It is your own tongue. It is not enough to be able to speak your own language—you have to know some of the literature. And you simply *must* have the basic structure of science. And with these three subjects, you must not be allowed to give them up before you are 16.... Now that is to me the core curriculum for every school. And it is so important that you simply *must* be tested on it. Going on to all the other things in the Curriculum—when we first started on this, I do not think I ever thought they would do the syllabus for each subject in such detail, as they are doing them now. The National Curriculum is becoming a national syllabus; and we are not leaving scope for teachers to use their own methods.... Now the

history Report has just come out.... My worry is whether we should put out such a detailed one. You see, once you put out an approved curriculum, if you have got it wrong, the situation is worse afterwards than it was before. (The Sunday Telegraph, April 15, 1990)

Changes to Key Stage Four under the Conservatives

With regard to the secondary school curriculum, the government's program for Key Stage Three remained virtually intact for the next 20 years, largely because it represented what most secondary schools were doing anyway; but the Key Stage Four curriculum for 14- to 16-year-olds was in the process of being abandoned, even before it was actually implemented.

The National Curriculum was, in fact, still very much in its infancy, when it became obvious to the education ministers appointed by John Major (1990–1997), that Key Stage Four could *not* survive in the form envisaged by the DES in 1987. Indeed, for a number of reasons, the last two years of compulsory schooling rapidly became the most problematic area of the Conservative government's curriculum and assessment program. There were the practical problems involved in fitting so many subjects and cross-curricular themes into a *finite* amount of curriculum time. Many teachers complained that it would be very difficult to teach all ten foundation subjects (together with religious education) to students of *all* abilities, without risking a fair amount of resentment and indiscipline. And as general economic prospects worsened, particularly after John Major's unexpected election victory in April 1992, there was renewed concern about the lack of qualified workers in Britain and a great deal of support for the idea that vocational courses should play a major role alongside "academic" subjects in the curriculum diet for many older students. Kenneth Baker and his advisers had thought in terms of a 5–16 curriculum, but there now seemed to be a case for planning courses and "curriculum pathways" as part of a 14–19 continuum.

The process of slimming down Key Stage Four began as early as the spring of 1991 when Education Secretary Kenneth Clarke (November 1990–April 1992) had decided to ignore the advice of the NCC (National Curriculum Council), and reduce the number of compulsory subjects. In his speech at the North of England Education Conference in Leeds in January, he made three important announcements:

(1) Only English, maths and science should remain "sacrosanct" in the last two years of formal schooling.
(2) Students would now be able to "drop" art, music, and history *or* geography, with physical education being treated "flexibly."
(3) All students would still have to study technology, together with a modern foreign language, in addition to the "core" subjects, but not necessarily to GCSE level.

The new structure was put forward as a victory for "common sense," and as a means of ensuring that once again schools would be in a position to cater to older students according to their various talents and differing job prospects. In the words of the education secretary:

> I believe we should not impose on our young people a rigid curriculum that leaves little scope for choice. By the age of 14, young people are beginning to look at what lies *beyond* compulsory schooling, whether in work or in further study. We must harness that sense of anticipation, if every student is to have the chance of developing to the full. (Reported in *The Guardian*, January 5, 1991)

For many curriculum experts, the idea of a narrow, subject-based curriculum for all 14- to 16-year-olds of the type specified in the 1988 act appeared as something of an *aberration*, with the government now being urged to offer youngsters a choice of discrete academic, technical, and vocational "pathways" at the age of 14.

Problems concerning the framework for Key Stage Four and the use of National Curriculum tests and examination tables drove the Major government to the realization that a full-scale review of the National Curriculum was called for; and to carry this out in a systematic fashion, it turned to Sir Ron Dearing, a former head of the post office, and the chairperson-designate of the new SCAA (School Curriculum and Assessment Authority), to be established in October 1993. The remit letter sent to Sir Ron Dearing on April 7 1993 listed "the scope for slimming down the Curriculum" as one of the major issues that had to be addressed by his review.

The final report of the so-called Dearing Review was published in January, 1994 (SCAA, 1994), and it recommended that the National

Curriculum at Key Stage Three should be cut back to no more than 80 percent of taught time, leaving the equivalent of at least a day a week for schools to use at their own discretion. At Key Stage Four, the curriculum could occupy students for only about 60 percent of the normal school week, assuming that the majority of students would choose to abide by no more than the *minimum* statutory requirement. The curriculum could still, in fact, take up between 70 and 80 percent of the school timetable if students opted to follow a double course in science and full examination courses in technology and a modern foreign language. The other subjects that constituted part of the minimum statutory requirement proposal included physical education, sex education, religious education, and careers.

The final report of the Dearing Review justified the abandonment of Key Stage Four in the form envisaged in 1987, on the grounds of "allowing greater scope for new academic and vocational options." It identified *three* broad pathways in post-16 education and training:

(1) the "craft" or "occupational," linked to NVQs (National Vocational Qualifications);
(2) the broadly "vocational," linked to GNVQs (General National Vocational Qualifications); and
(3) the "academic," leading to "A" and "AS" Levels.

It was recognized that the development of these three broad "pathways" raised the issue of whether younger students (those aged 14–16) should be allowed to follow a well-devised vocational course as *one* element in a broadly based curriculum. In the words of the final report:

> It will be a particular challenge to establish how a vocational pathway, which maintains a broad educational component, might be developed at Key Stage Four over the next few years, as part of a broad 14-to-19 continuum.... Such a pathway is already a feature in many European countries; and secondary headteachers and others have clearly indicated their interest in the opportunities which these courses can offer to young people. (SCAA, 1994, p. 47)

The report went on to recommend that the School Curriculum and Assessment Authority (SCAA) should be asked to work "closely and urgently" with the National Council for Vocational Qualifications (NCVQ), to identify whether a number of possibilities concerning GNVQs could now be developed (p. 49).

And in an address to the Secondary Heads Association's Annual Conference meeting in Bournemouth in March 1994. Sir Ron Dearing announced that 14-year-old students would soon be able to study for qualifications in one or other of five vocational areas:

(1) manufacturing;
(2) art and design;
(3) health and social care;
(4) leisure and tourism;
(5) business and finance.

(Reported in *The Financial Times*, March 21, 1994)

If we can sum up the rather complex developments outlined in this section: by the time the Conservatives left office in 1997, the Key Stage Four curriculum bore little resemblance to the framework devised ten years earlier by Kenneth Baker. All maintained secondary schools in England and Wales were now required to teach the relevant programs of study in the following subjects (with Welsh as an additional "core" subject for pupils in those parts of Wales where Welsh was spoken): English, mathematics, science (as a "single" or "double" program, although with the clear expectation that more "able" students would choose to take "double science"), design and technology (with a short course being the minimum requirement), information technology (as a separate subject or coordinated across other subjects), a modem foreign language, and physical education. There was no place for history, geography, art, and music as compulsory subjects. Secondary schools also had a statutory duty to provide religious education, in accordance with a locally agreed syllabus, and a program of carefully structured sex education. Careers education was scheduled to become a statutory part of the secondary curriculum from September 1998.

New Labour Changes to the Secondary Curriculum

The National Curriculum at Key Stage Three attracted comparatively little attention from New Labour education ministers during the ten-year period of the Blair government (1997–2007), although there was an attempt at intervention from Education Secretary Estelle Morris in 2002. Giving a published talk to a group of teachers and educationists at an event in London, hosted by the think tank Demos, on March 21, 2002, Ms. Morris declared her intention to tackle the quality of the learning experience for 11- to 14-year-old pupils, which she described as "one of the long-neglected and toughest challenges facing our secondary schools today" (Morris, 2002a, p. 3). The education secretary expressed her anxiety that while large numbers of pupils were leaving their primary school with "a great sense of confidence, excitement and eager anticipation," there was invariably "a great fall-off in their attitude to learning" in the first year at their new secondary school. She described the problem in these terms:

> The majority of eleven-year-olds arrive in their new secondary school really proud of their achievements at primary level, and keen to build on those and play more of an active role in their own learning, with an appetite to learn new skills and extend their horizons.... Yet in the past, we have too often failed to capitalize on that enthusiasm, and not done enough to fire their imagination, and stretch their ambitions. Most secondary schools have tended to focus their efforts on later examination classes; and teaching in the middle years has sometimes lacked pace and focus. (Morris, 2002a, pp. 4–5)

In the view of Estelle Morris, the secondary school system was generally too uniform, and too inflexible in its approach to change. As we saw in chapter 5, she was of the firm opinion that comprehensive schools had concentrated all their energies on developing their essential sameness and had failed to offer their pupils an education tailored to individual needs. The answer put forward in her Demos speech was to provide a greater variety of secondary schools, and to lay a stronger emphasis on raising the expectations of all pupils, through stretching "the more able," while providing additional help for those who were "clearly struggling." Building a more secure platform of achievement, motivation, and engagement with learning by the end of Key Stage Three would then provide schools with the springboard needed for "the greater choice and range of opportunities envisaged for 14- to-19-year-old students" (Morris, 2002a, p. 6).

Five years later, on July 12, 2007, the government, now led by Gordon Brown, revealed details of a new plan for the Key Stage Three curriculum, to be introduced in September 2008, which was intended to "free-up" 25 percent of the school timetable. This "slimmed-down" curriculum was designed to liberate more time to help pupils, either to "catch up on the basics" or to "play to their strengths." The changes were said to be in line with the government's "personalized learning agenda," and to reflect anxieties both about the continuing "tail of underachievement" in secondary schools, and about the large number of "able" pupils who were not being "pushed hard enough, early enough." Speaking at the launch of this revised curriculum at a press conference in London, Schools Minister Lord Adonis said: "there will now be a clear reduction in prescription from the Centre and a modernization of the Key Stage Three Curriculum, to make it more relevant to the needs of young people in this world in the future." Teachers would be encouraged to use the new time, either to arrange "extra catch-up lessons in the three Rs for those pupils who were struggling," or to devise exciting new lessons to stretch the "more able" (reported in *The Independent*, July 13, 2007).

Where Key Stage Four was concerned, New Labour was keen to continue with the policy, advocated by Sir Ron Dearing, of viewing curriculum provision for older students in terms of a 14–19 "continuum." And this concept received very strong support in the green paper *14–19: Extending Opportunities, Raising Standards*, which was published in February 2002 (DfES, 2002). Indeed, one of the main themes to emerge from this important consultation document was that the 14–19 period should be treated as "a single phase," with all students being encouraged to move "at a pace best suited to their abilities and preferred ways of learning" (p. 29). The paper set out an evolving vision for far greater coherence in the 14–19 phase of education and training in England, whereby the age of 16 would lose its status as "a traditional break-point" in the lives of young students. In the words of the document, "We need to transform the age of 16 from the point at which young people divide into those who stay on and those who leave, into the point where every young person is committed to continuing to learn" (p. 7).

In her Foreword to the 2002 green paper, Education and Skills Secretary Estelle Morris repeated the familiar refrain that, in the second half of the twentieth century, "the education system was too often a 'one-size-fits-all' structure." The need for reform of the 14–19 secondary school curriculum has never been more urgent; and there are four "central challenges" that the country has to address, if we are to guarantee "economic prosperity and social justice for all in the new century":

(1) to build an education system, in which every young person and every parent has confidence;
(2) to ensure that no young person is denied the chance of a decent education;
(3) to reap the skills benefits of an education system that matches the needs of the knowledge economy;
(4) to promote education with "character," meaning that while academic achievement is essential, education must also be a basis for citizenship and inclusion. (pp. 4–5)

Chapter 1 of the green paper outlined the scale of the problem that had to be tackled. Only three out of four 16-to 18-year-olds in England were in full-time education and training at the end of 2000; and, although this figure had been steadily rising in recent years, it was still worrying that it remained well *below* European and OECD averages. In 2001, around 5 percent of young people did not achieve any GCSE passes at all, and although the proportion of Year 11 students gaining five or more A* to C grades at GCSE had risen dramatically since 1997, it still accounted for only 50 percent of the cohort. Perhaps of greatest concern was the fact that less than 20 percent of young people under the age of 21 from the lowest socioeconomic groups went on to some form of higher education, compared with over 70 percent from the highest. All these dismal statistics had to be viewed in the context of one of the government's major targets: to increase and broaden participation in higher education so that, by the end of the decade, around 50 percent of those aged between 18 and 30 would be going to university, with access widened, in particular, for those whose families could claim no previous experience of any form of higher education. In the words of the green paper: "Getting the proper representation of students from low-income families in higher education depends heavily on transforming their experience of the 14-to-19 phase in school, college, or workplace" (p. 11).

Chapter 3 of the green paper made the case for a new structure for the National Curriculum at Stage Four. This involved a further "slimming down" of the curriculum, so that it would now comprise a fairly limited core of "compulsory" subjects: mathematics, English, science, and ICT (Information and Communications Technology), alongside citizenship, religious education, careers education, sex education, physical education, and work-related learning. Modem foreign languages and design and technology would no longer be "required study" for *all* students; but they would now join the arts and the humanities as subjects where, in the words of the document, there would be "a new statutory entitlement of access" (p. 20). And the government's decision to make French, German, and other modem European languages "optional" at Key Stage Four would be "offset," by the introduction of a foreign language into the primary-school curriculum at Key Stage Two.

The 2002 green paper received a good deal of media publicity; and it was these new "slimming down" proposals that provoked great anxiety among many teachers and commentators. Although it was made clear that the decision to make both foreign languages and design and technology "optional" for 14- to 16-year-olds would *not* be implemented until September 2004, there was evidence to suggest that large numbers of secondary schools were prepared to risk breaking the law by dropping these subjects as part of the "compulsory" provision with immediate effect. Figures from a survey carried out on behalf of the Association of Language Learning (ALL), and reported in *The Times Educational Supplement* on May 24, 2002, revealed that around 30 percent of the secondary schools canvassed planned to abandon compulsory language lessons for their older students as early as the Autumn of 2002. And it was especially worrying that the majority of the schools planning to dispense with compulsory language courses were those situated in deprived inner-city areas, giving rise to fears among teachers that learning a foreign language, such as French or German, to an advanced level could soon be viewed as an "elitist" activity, confined to largely middle-class suburban areas. The government's decision to "compensate" for its decision at Key Stage Four by offering primary-school pupils a new "entitlement" to a modem foreign language at Key Stage Two, was dismissed by ALL president Terry Lamb as "a half-hearted fudge," designed purely to "deflect criticism from the post-14 proposal."

It is worth noting that the attempt to gauge reaction to the green paper was one of the most extensive consultation exercises ever carried out by the education department. The DfES received as many as 2,000 written responses to its consultation document; and a series of informal events involving young students from schools and colleges throughout the country resulted in the receipt of a further 4,000 written replies.

During the Summer of 2002, representatives of every secondary school and of every FE (Further Education) college in England, as well as a wide range of other so-called stakeholders, were invited to one or other of 58 regional 14–19 workshops managed jointly by LEAs and LSCs (Learning and Skills Councils), where all the main ideas in the green paper were thrown open to discussion. The result of all this consultation was the publication, on January 21, 2003, of a new discussion document: *14–19: Opportunity and Excellence* (DfES, 2003). In his Foreword to this new discussion document, Education and Skills Secretary Charles Clarke (October 2002–December 2004) reiterated the Government's commitment to the concept of a 14–19 "continuum"—that "critical phase" in young people's lives when "they build on their earlier learning and prepare for adult life and employment." It was that critical period when, in Clarke's words, "all students need a coherent and motivating curriculum, delivered in a wide range of institutions, recognized and assessed by a coherent qualifications system" (p. 3).

To attain the government's objectives, it was necessary to distinguish between *short-term* and *long-term* reforms, many of the former having been foreshadowed in earlier discussion documents.

Where the Key Stage Four curriculum was concerned, it had been decided to ignore advice that modern foreign languages and design and technology should be reinstated as "compulsory" subjects. From the *2004–2005* academic year onwards, English, mathematics, and science would be the only academic "survivors" from Kenneth Baker's original 1987 framework. All 14-year-old students would learn about work and enterprise; and ICT would remain compulsory *for the time being*, though with the understanding that the skills involved here would eventually be taught *through other subjects*. Citizenship, religious education, sex education, physical education, and careers education would remain as compulsory elements in the curriculum, but even with these subjects there was "clear potential for greater co-ordination and cross-curriculum delivery" than was currently the case (p. 20). The emphasis throughout would be on flexibility and choice.

With regard to *long-term* strategy, the most important announcement in the document was that the government would be setting up a new working group for 14–19 reform, headed by Mike Tomlinson, former chief inspector for schools. One of its main tasks would be to look at ways of introducing a sort of English Baccalaureate, a "grouped award" like the French Baccalaureate or the German Arbitur, designed to recognize a broad range of academic and vocational achievements, as well as worthwhile activities outside the classroom, such as volunteering, and catering to *all* students across the so-called "ability" spectrum. In the words of the document:

> Baccalaureate-style qualifications of this type obviously work well in other countries; and we believe that this new model, designed to suit English circumstances, could tackle long-standing English problems, giving greater emphasis to completing courses of study (and training as appropriate), through to the age of 18 or 19, but without a heavier burden on examination and assessment....A change to this type of model would be a *long-term* reform, but one on which we are quite ready to embark, if further work shows that such a unified system can prepare our students for the varied needs of higher education and employment. This sort of reform needs to be carefully planned and built on consensus, as will be recommended by Mitt Tomlinson's Report....We are committed to work with all the partners interested in the future of 14-to-19 education, to test whether we can, in fact, achieve consensus on a workable model, that can be developed for implementation. (DfES, 2003, p. 13)

The Tomlinson Report

The final report of the working group headed by Mike Tomlinson did not appear until October 2004, but its main proposals did not come as a complete surprise, since preliminary details of the reforms advocated by the group had appeared in the media as early as July 2003. It had been confidently predicted that the report would favor the introduction of a broad "baccalaureate-style" diploma, comprising *four* levels of difficulty. The entry level would be equivalent to the standard expected of most students at the age of 14 at the start of Key Stage Four; while foundation level would be the same as achieving the lower grades in the GCSE examination. Then the intermediate level would be roughly equivalent to achieving at least five GCSE passes at grade C or above; and the advanced level would equate with existing A Levels. It was not clear at that stage what would happen to existing GCSEs and A Levels: was it Tomlinson's intention that they would be abolished; or would they survive as component parts of the new diploma, rather than as free-standing qualifications?

It was on October 18, 2004 that Mike Tomlinson's final report, *14–19 Curriculum and Qualifications Reform*, was published; and, on the day before, in *The Observer* (October 17, 2004), it was confidently asserted that acceptance of the main Tomlinson proposals would constitute "the biggest shake-up of the examinations system in England in over half a century." On the day of publication itself, Rebecca Smithers, the education editor of *The Guardian*, predicted that the main ideas in the report would appear in New Labour's manifesto for the 2005 general election. While ministers would probably delay a "substantive response" to the blueprint to replace GCSEs and A Levels with "a new over-arching diploma," they would back "the overall concept of the reforms," which would be "fleshed out" in a white paper and then "feature in the 2005 Manifesto" (*The Guardian*, October 18, 2004). In a letter to Secretary of State Charles Clarke, included as an introduction to the final report, Mike Tomlinson claimed that the 116-page document set out "a clear vision for a unified framework of 14–19 curriculum and qualifications." One of the main aims of his working group had been to bring back "a passion for learning"; and it was hoped that all learners would be enabled to achieve "as highly as possible" with all their achievements being recognized. In the words of the letter, "We must ensure rigour, and that all young people are equipped with the knowledge, skills, and attributes needed for HE, employment and adult life."

As foreshadowed back in July 2003, the main reform advocated in the report was that existing GCSEs and A Levels should form part of a new wide-ranging diploma. It would indeed be made up of *four* levels: two of them below the level of good GCSEs, an intermediate level corresponding to five good GCSE passes, and an advanced diploma intended for A Level standard students. It was expected that all 14-year-old students would be able to choose from around 20 "lines of learning" within the overall diploma framework, consisting of either academic or vocational subjects, or a mixture of the two. Each student's final diploma would also take account of work experience and extracurricular activities. To placate all those who still regarded A Levels as the "gold standard," the highest level of diploma would be assessed largely by external examination papers, and new A plus and A double plus grades would be introduced to "stretch" the ablest students. It was hoped that this would satisfy the "Russell Group" of elite universities, who wanted to be able to identify the "brightest" candidates among a large group of

A Level success stories. At a briefing in London on October 18, 2004, Mike Tomlinson accepted that GCSEs and A Levels *could* form part of his new diploma framework, though ideally as "components," rather than as "surviving free-standing qualifications." But he also added that he hoped that these names would "eventually disappear," so that the new diploma would acquire "full integrity." "If you kept these names," he said, "it would clearly deny the fact that there is an inherent integrity in the Diploma. This is a very subtle point, but it is also an important one" (reported in *The Guardian*, October 19, 2004).

As it happened, Mike Tomlinson's optimism turned out to be cruelly misplaced; and, even as he spoke, Tony Blair and his education secretary were desperately seeking to distance themselves from the report's main conclusions. Speaking to the Confederation of British Industry at a meeting in Birmingham, the prime minister was anxious to stress that GCSEs and A Levels would not disappear during his period in office:

> The purpose of reform will be to improve upon the existing system, *not* replace it.... GCSEs and A Levels will stay, and so will all externally marked exams. Reform will serve to strengthen the existing system where it is inadequate, and there will be greater challenge at the top for those on track to Higher Education. There will also be a sharper focus on the basics of literacy and numeracy and ICT. And there will also be an improved vocational provision. (Reported in *The Guardian*, October 19, 2004)

In this well-publicized speech, Tony Blair stopped far short of giving the Tomlinson Report his unequivocal endorsement. Introducing the Tomlinson Report in the House of Commons on October 18, Education Secretary Charles Clarke gave it lukewarm praise, and some of his more cautious comments reflected concern among ministers and civil servants that a fair amount of assessment at the intermediate level of the proposed diploma—that is, the equivalent of good GCSE passes—could be carried out *internally* by teachers. There was no suggestion that A Levels and GCSEs would be replaced in any sort of major "shake-up," and this is what he said:

> I am determined that any evolution of the 14-to-19 system must increase public confidence in it. My approach will be to build on all that is good in the current system—including the real and great strengths of A Levels

and GCSEs. They will stay as the essential building-blocks of any new system.... At the same time, assessment *must* and *will* continue, at all levels, on the basis of rigorous, trusted and externally-marked examinations, although we will probably need to consider the number and nature of these exams. (Reported in *The Guardian*, October 19, 2004)

When Education Secretary Ruth Kelly (December 2004–May 2006) published her department's new white paper on the 14–19 curriculum,) *14–19 Education and Skills* on February 23, 2005 (DfES, 2005a), it was obvious that the Blair government had no intention of carrying out a major overhaul of provision for older students so close to an impending general election. In her Foreword to the white paper, the new education secretary argued that the white paper set out the details of a major reform program, "building from the excellent work of Sir Mike Tomlinson and his Working Group on 14–19 Reform" (p. 3), while the 93-page document itself rejected most of Tomlinson's key proposals. Above all, it rejected the working party's idea of a four-tier overarching diploma incorporating all existing academic and vocational qualifications, and opted instead to retain A Levels and GCSEs largely in their present form. It did accept the need for a major rationalization of all existing vocational qualifications, with the replacement of the "alphabet soup" of around 3,500 separate qualifications, by a three-tier system of "specialized diplomas" in 14 occupational areas (p. 53). The first four diplomas, in information and communication technology, engineering, health and social care, and creative studies and media would be made available in 2008. A further four would be available in 2010, and diplomas would become "a national entitlement" by the year 2015. In order to complete any of these diplomas, a young person would need to demonstrate at the appropriate level:

- a core of functional skills in both English and maths;
- specialized learning in the relevant discipline;
- suitable work experience; and
- any relevant GCSEs or A Levels (for example, the science necessary for understanding engineering).

Diplomas had to be constructed out of a number of units, and it was essential that the combination of units taken really did provide "the sort of preparation that employers and universities were looking for" (p. 50).

It was a cause of much concern among members of the education community that the government was prepared to rule out diplomas for "academic" courses; and *The Guardian* and *The Daily Telegraph* talked in terms of "outcry" among teachers' leaders at the limited nature of the reforms outlined in the new white paper. Why had Ruth Kelly chosen to reject the two most important (though controversial) proposals in Mike Tomlinson's report: the overarching diploma intended to establish genuine "parity of esteem" between the academic and vocational routes; and the phasing out of A Levels and GCSEs? Mike Tomlinson himself warned that the short-sighted decision to opt for diplomas solely for vocational courses—while keeping the existing "gold standard" examinations—could easily "backfire on the Government by prolonging and reinforcing the traditional snobbery towards work-related education." He went on:

> What is being proposed risks emphasizing yet again the distinction between the vocational and the academic. It further fails fully to deal with the needs of those students for whom grade A* to C at GCSE is simply not attainable.... While the new White Paper leaves one or two doors still open—for example, a review of coursework—and introduces welcome new diplomas, I had hoped that the Government would have gone further on the need for a unified qualifications framework. This was, after all, a key part of the brief given to my Working Group, yet the White Paper makes little or no direct reference to such a framework. (Reported in *The Guardian*, February 24, 2005)

David Bell, the chief inspector of schools, also argued that "continuing with the current A Level and GCSE structure carries the risk of continuing the historic divide between academic and vocational courses, which has ill-served too many young people in the past" (ibid.). John Dunford, general secretary of the Secondary Heads Association, said: "The limited reforms announced today will do very little for those who have hitherto been failed by the qualifications system. Electoral tactics, it seems, have taken precedence over educational logic" (ibid). And education journalist Warwick Mansell, writing in *The Times Educational Supplement* on February 25, 2005, argued that "all the attention given to the 14 to 19 age group, including the £1 million Tomlinson Inquiry, appears to have been rejected because the Government does not want to go into the 2005 General Election being accused by the Tories and the right-wing media of scrapping A Levels" (Mansell, 2005).

It was not until 2007 that Ed Balls, who had been given the post of schools secretary in the newly created Department of Children, Schools and Families when Gordon Brown took over from Tony Blair as prime minister in June, revisited the whole issue of 14–19 reform and appeared to signal a major change in government thinking, in an important speech to a meeting in London delivered on October 23. It was immediately clear that the government had had second thoughts about some of the main proposals in the Tomlinson Report. Mr. Balls was flanked on the platform by (Sir) Mike Tomlinson and Richard Lambert, director general of the CBI (Confederation of British Industry). Once again, the government's proposals were hailed by sections of the media as "the biggest shake-up of the examinations system in over half a century"— but this time, the hyperbole appeared to have some justification. It was announced that five diplomas would be introduced in September 2008 in about nine hundred schools and colleges, covering construction, engineering, media, IT and society, and health and development. This much was clearly in line with the sort of government thinking outlined in the 2005 white paper; but Ed Balls went much further, by stressing that in the future, new diplomas would no longer be restricted to specifically vocational or work-related areas of the curriculum. Three new diplomas, in languages, sciences, and humanities, would be launched in September 2011, in a move designed to appeal to "academic" sixth-form students and the universities. As more and more "academic" diplomas were introduced, they would compete with many existing "academic" examinations, and it was clearly hoped that they could well become the "qualification of choice" for 14- to 19-year olds. In the words of the schools secretary himself: "The new Diplomas could become "the jewel in the crown" of the education system. A review of A Levels, expected to take place in 2008, would be postponed to 2013 and would be expanded to cover all qualifications. Asked by members of the audience on October 23, whether he could give a guarantee that A Levels and GCSEs would actually survive this review, Ed Balls replied: "It will be an open-minded review. Clearly, I'm not going to give you any guarantee about the outcome of the 2013 Review." And all this gave rise to a headline in *The Times* (October 24, 2007), which read: "A Levels Face Axe in Favour of Diplomas."

Not surprisingly, the schools secretary's speech had a mixed reception. Sir Mike Tomlinson was able to welcome the expansion of diplomas; and Richard Lambert said he was pleased that the postponement of the 2008 review would allow adequate time for a thorough discussion of the government's new initiative. The new diplomas were welcomed by several big businesses, including Land Rover, Vodafone, and British Telecom. And it was announced that at least seven universities, including Leeds and Nottingham, would accept the engineering diploma as a way on to the relevant degree courses. John Dunford, the general secretary of the Association of School and College Leaders (formerly the Secondary Heads Association) welcomed the proposals, but was concerned about the workload involved. In his view, "adding three more (academic) Diplomas to the 14 already under construction in schools and colleges, and against the backdrop of continuing to provide all the traditional GCSE and A Level courses, is a huge programme for an education system that is simply punch-drunk with change in recent years" (quoted in *The Times*, October 24, 2007).

Michael Gove, the shadow schools secretary, was predictably hostile to everything he heard in the Balls speech. He said that the new diplomas in academic subjects would serve to "undermine the traditional qualifications"; He went on: "Diplomas were supposed to be about *improving* vocational education not *undermining* academic excellence.... We support the reform of vocational learning, but these new exams are clearly designed to subvert GCSEs and A Levels" (quoted in *The Times*, October 27, 2007).

The Brown government was very anxious that the new diploma system would be a success, thereby finally ending the long-standing divide between academic and vocational learning. A clause in the new Education and Skills Bill, introduced into parliament on January 14, 2008, specified that henceforth, secondary schools would be forbidden from "unduly promoting any particular options" to teenagers seeking advice on suitable courses; and this was widely seen as a thinly disguised attempt to prevent teachers from encouraging older students to follow A Level options.

But it was actually the issue of timing that was the main problem for the future of "academic" diplomas. It was obvious, for example, that by the year 2013, when the review of A Levels was scheduled to take place, there would have to be a general election. If the Conservatives were successful, and bearing in mind Michael Gove's immediate reaction to Ed Balls's speech, A Levels would undoubtedly remain *outside* any diploma framework. The change of heart over the Tomlinson Report had come too late in the narrative of the New Labour administration; and those traditionalists who were in favor of the old regime were to benefit from the government's timidity and prevarication.

* * *

Conclusion

We have seen that New Labour was keen to continue with the policy of John Major's government in amending and reformulating the original structure of the National Curriculum, particularly at Key Stage Four, dealing with the needs of 14- to 16-year-old students. The statutory curriculum was effectively reduced to a limited "core" of traditional disciplines (maths, English, and science), while new and seemingly more "relevant" subjects were added to the mix with students afforded a greater degree of choice at the age of 14. At the same time, though rather late in the day, the Brown government was prepared to experiment with the idea of an English Baccalaureate, with GCSE and A Level examinations being slowly phased out in favor of a system of diplomas covering both academic and vocational options. This idea was strongly opposed by the Conservative opposition, and was destined to be shelved when New Labour lost the 2010 general election.

Chapter 8

International Perspectives

Introduction

The changes affecting secondary education in Britain, or perhaps more accurately in England, outlined in this book, and concentrating on the period of the three New Labour administrations between 1997 and 2010, were *not* isolated phenomena peculiar to one country, and can therefore be usefully viewed in the context of much broader international developments. In particular, the privatization of secondary education, which has been such a notable feature of the educational scene in England in recent years, and which has assumed many different forms, has had distinct parallels in a number of other countries, with profound and sometimes unforeseen consequences for the future of education as a "public good." This process has been accompanied by a growing disillusionment with the comprehensive model as ideal for the future of secondary state schooling, a model which seemed in many countries to carry all before it in the period after the end of the Second World War. This chapter will begin by examining the changes that have occurred since 1945 in the perception of the comprehensive high school as the most suitable institution for the education of adolescents in advanced industrialized societies.

Historical Perspectives

In *Half Way There*, their 1970 report on the British comprehensive school reform already referred to in chapter 3, Caroline Benn and Brian

Simon argued that, generally speaking, the more backward a nation was economically, the more heavily committed it was to a highly segregated secondary school system—and this was to be expected, since opportunities for the employment of the educated were few. For too long, Britain had been committed to a wasteful system of differentiated schools, providing alternative forms of education at the secondary stage; It now stood at the crossroads, at the half-way mark in the creation of a new system, "half realizing the need for, but still fearing the consequences of, a radical break with tradition." In its uncertainty over which path to pursue, it had failed to recognize that there had been a general movement toward providing a common secondary education *for all* in so many parts of the world—and, in particular, in the United States. If placed in an international context, recent developments in Britain appeared simply as a special instance of a *universal* trend, which could itself be seen as a response to a new scientific and technological revolution. In the words of Benn and Simon, the movement toward comprehensive secondary education was clearly not "peculiar to Britain alone"; it was, in fact, "part of a worldwide movement concerned to adapt the structure of secondary education to the new demands of scientific, technological, social, racial, and cultural progress" (Benn and Simon, 1970, p. 13).

In their follow-up study *Thirty Years on: Is Comprehensive Education Alive and Well or Struggling to Survive?* first published in 1996, Caroline Benn and Clyde Chitty also argued that the move toward comprehensive secondary schooling in Britain was part of a worldwide evolutionary process. They argued that "there may well be individual exceptions that prove the rule, but it is true that, in general, most countries start off with highly selective systems and gradually translate to broadly comprehensive ones as they move up the industrializing scale—and particularly if they wish to compete at the top" (Benn and Chitty, 1996; 1997, p. 20). This did *not* mean that many countries did not also have exclusive, private secondary schools for a tiny international clientele, although, as Brian Simon has noted, Britain is "the only advanced industrial country in the world that boasts two distinct systems—one for the wealthier and more privileged, and the other for the rest" (Simon, 1994, p. 66). It did, however, mean that where public money was used to finance education for the majority, "the long-term aim has to be organization up to the age of adult specialization, without institutionalizing any form of social or attainment selection."

Benn and Chitty also argued that "comprehensive education was not a form of schooling practised exclusively by societies governed by the Left." It was equally at home in societies governed by right-wing capitalist principles, a fact that many right-wing Conservative politicians in Britain still found it difficult to accept. Most European politicians would be staggered to read the following comments by Nick Hawkins, the Conservative MP for Blackpool South, interrupting a statement by Labour education spokesperson David Blunkett, in a heated education debate in the House of Commons in February 1995:

> Does the Hon. Gentleman not realise that the fact that so few of our 14-year-olds reach the required educational standard is largely a result of the mad, doctrinaire, Socialist ideas of comprehensivization, and the vast waste of money in Labour-run local education authorities?... That is surely why so many secondary schools want to opt out of local authority control: to ensure that better resources are targeted directly to pupils, and not wasted by Labour-run local education authorities. (*Hansard*, H. of C., Vol. 254, cols. 151–52, February 7, 1995).

Reflecting on this statement, Benn and Chitty commented in their 1996 study:

> This continuing failure to read world reality hampers any party or government within a world where implementation of the comprehensive principle in some form or other is an *integral* part of modernizing an industrialized society, capable of adaptation by capitalist, socialist and liberal regimes, alike. This principle is incompatible *only* with hierarchically organized tribal or feudal societies, which seek to regulate themselves by inherited social or economic authority, or with those societies where cultural, social or racial segregation is practiced within a rule of one dominant culture, rather than within a diversity of *equally valued* groups and cultures.... In the long run, however, it may also be true that *full* comprehensive education, in any meaningful sense, is simply not possible in those societies in the world where a basic form of democracy does not also exist. And this follows from its defining social inclusiveness, its place in the community, its rationality, and its belief in the inherent educability of everyone. (Benn and Chitty, 1996, p. 21)

Writing in 2007, Barry Franklin and Gary McCulloch took issue with the sentiments expressed by Benn, Chitty, and Simon in the preceding paragraphs. In challenging their rather simplistic view of the international dimension to the story of the comprehensive high school, they argued that different nations and regions would appear to have developed in ways that were more "complex and varied." Moreover, "the social and political challenges of recent years have made it less than clear whether this one best system will survive unscathed, much less that it will prosper, and dominate the scene across the board" (Franklin and McCulloch, 2007, p. 202).

It is a point of some significance that at the time when the research for *Thirty Years On* was being undertaken, forces inimical to the future of the comprehensive high school were acquiring global significance. An advertisement that appeared in *The Times Educational Supplement* on February 2, 1990, for the 1990 International Privatization Congress to be held in Saskatchewan, Canada, in May 1990, began with the following ringing declaration:

> Historians will certainly record the ninth decade of the twentieth century and the accelerating developments of the final months of 1989 as a transitional period in the global political economy. The unexpected collapse of the one-party system in Eastern Europe and the resultant drive for a return to market-driven economies capped a decade, which has seen governments worldwide, and of all political stripes, embark on substantial privatization programmes.

No mention was made of education as such, but privatization options were to be considered with regard to government services, health care, housing, transportation, and numerous other areas of social policy.

We have already seen in chapter 6 that throughout the 1980s, and particularly after 1987, the Thatcher government in Britain displayed a marked preference for more privatized, competitive, and market-oriented forms of welfare and education provision. And a loss of confidence in public enterprises was certainly not confined to the United Kingdom. A change in attitude toward the funding and provision of education was commented upon by Edwards, Fitz, and Whitty in an article published in 1985:

> In most advanced industrial societies, schooling has long been a predominantly public enterprise.... Only in a very few countries...has the major part of secondary education traditionally been delegated to "nonpublic" institutions, aided by massive public subsidies.... In the past few years, however, a loss of confidence in public enterprises in

general, and in state education in particular, has led people all over the world, to call into question the very assumption that education is best conceived as a compulsory and universal service, both financed and provided by governments. In many countries, the reductions in government spending on education in response to recession have been accompanied by a marked withdrawal of political support from the public sector. Overt displays of a lack of confidence may be no more than pragmatic adjustments to a declining belief in the wealth-creating and opportunity-creating effects of schooling. Often, however, they have been expressions of a political preference for greater consumer choice or for a transfer of more of the cost of services to their users, or an assertion of belief in the particular capacity of the private sector to maintain academic standards and social values judged to be in real danger outside it. (Edwards, Fitz, and Whitty, 1985, p. 29)

It seems clear that the social and economic world has been transformed in a number of significant ways since the early 1980s. So how have the education systems of some of the major industrialized nations in the world responded to the global trends of the past three decades? This is the question we will attempt to address in the following sections of this chapter.

Comparative Perspectives

As Benn and Simon noted back in 1970, the United States played a pioneering role in the movement toward providing a common secondary education for all in the period following the end of the Second World War. Indeed, *Half Way There* (1970) was originally conceived as a counterpart to James Conant's influential reports on the American comprehensive high school. Looking at the situation in the United States, Benn and Simon acknowledged the real power of the twin ideals of "equality of opportunity" and "equality of status," and it seemed evident that the American people had come to believe that enhanced educational opportunity for all provided the means by which these twin ideals were to be realized. Already by 1910, the American high schools were taking in around 35 percent of youngsters aged 17 and over, and by the end of the 1950s, this figure had risen to well over 70 percent (Benn and Simon, 1970, p. 6).

In one of his most acclaimed texts, *The American High School Today: A First Report to Interested Citizens*, published in 1959, Dr. Conant felt able to claim that "the American public high school has become an institution, which has no counterpart in any other country." With few exceptions, largely confined to large eastern cities, this type of secondary school was expected to provide "an appropriate education for *all* the youth living in a town, city, or district" (Conant, 1959, p. 7). Dr. Conant then went on to make a number of significant points:

> Though generalization about American public education is highly dangerous... I believe it accurate to state that a high school accommodating all the youth of a community is typical of American public education. I think it safe to say that the comprehensive high school is characteristic of our society and, further, that it has come into being because of our economic history and our devotion to the ideals of equality of opportunity and equality of status. (Conant, 1959, p. 8)

But, writing 50 years later, and commenting on the contemporary scene, Franklin and McCulloch felt able to challenge the longevity of at least *three* of Dr. Conant's main assertions: "The extent to which the comprehensive high school accommodated *all* the youth of a particular community; the notion that it was somehow characteristic of American society; and the idea that it had *no* counterpart in any other country" (Franklin and McCulloch, 2007, p. 202).

It can still be argued today that the wide accessibility of the comprehensive high school in America has made it the preeminent instrument for advancing the cause of equal opportunity in America, and ultimately that of American democracy itself. While conceding that there was "no such thing as a *typical* American high school" and that it would be "quite impossible to draw up a blueprint for the *ideal* high school," Dr. Conant concluded his 1959 report by anticipating that his proposals for American secondary education could be successful in all parts of the United States, but *only* if "the citizens in all the various localities displayed sufficient interest in their schools and were willing to support them" (Conant, 1959, p. 96). Since these words were written, it is not clear that public support for this type of secondary school has been there in all instances. Many have been highly critical of the high school's attempt to cater to everyone, arguing that the effort of high school leaders to provide for *all* the students in a locality has led to the establishment of a bewildering multitude of programs, and the delivery of a fragmented curriculum that lacks a unified purpose and focus. At the same time, there has been the familiar refrain, also much in evidence in England, that any attempt to create an institution that is responsive to the needs of *all* students leads inevitably to the abandonment of academic rigor and high standards.

After his election as president in November 1980, and being very much influenced by the ideas of libertarian economist Milton Friedman, Ronald Reagan was very keen to promote choice and diversity in the American education system. As early as 1955, Friedman had published an essay, "The Role of Government in Education," recommending that the government should issue a voucher to all parents, which they could cash in at any school of their choice—whether run by a religious order, a "for-profit" business, a "non-profit" agency, or a public authority—provided that the school could be shown to meet "specified minimum standards" (Friedman, 1955). Reagan shared Friedman's emphasis on choice, freedom, deregulation, market-based solutions, and privatization; and Friedman actually became one of the president's close advisers. In actual fact, privatizing initiatives met with limited success in the 1980s, but it was at this time that the concept of school choice found a home among a number of right-wing, free market-oriented foundations and think tanks, which gave birth to a whole generation of academics and journalists who advocated market-driven approaches to schooling long after the end of the Reagan administration in 1989.

In 1990, a book was published by an independent organization called the Brookings Institution: *Politics, Markets, and America's Schools*, by John E. Chubb and Terry M. Moe, which was to exert a powerful influence on both Republican and Democratic politicians. The authors argued, provocatively, that the political institutions which governed America's schools functioned "naturally and routinely, despite everyone's best intentions, to burden the schools with excessive bureaucracy, to inhibit effective organization, and to stifle student achievement." In fact, poor student performance was "one of the prices Americans had to pay for choosing to exercise direct democratic control over their schools." So long as state schools were subject to democratic control, a number of powerful interest groups would work hard to protect the *status quo*, and the schools could never be improved. In the view of Chubb and Moe, the powerful groups with vested interest in preserving the current institutional framework consisted of: teachers' unions, and myriad associations of school principals, school boards, superintendents, administrators, and professionals—not to mention teacher training schools, book publishers, testing services, and all the other beneficiaries of the American system" (Chubb and Moe, 1990, pp. 2, 12).

The only way to bring about meaningful change in schooling, and especially secondary schooling, was through a system of school choice. Serious reformers had to entertain the notion that choice *was* a panacea. In the words of Chubb and Moe:

> Choice is not like other reforms, and should *not* be combined with other measures as part of a reformist strategy for improving America's public schools. Choice is a self-contained reform, with its own rationale and justification. It has the capacity, *all by itself*, to bring about the kind of transformation that, for years, reformers have been seeking to engineer in myriad other ways.... The whole point of a thoroughgoing system of school choice is to free the schools from all kinds of disabling constraints, by sweeping away the old institutions, and replacing them with new ones. Taken seriously, choice is not a *system-preserving* reform. It is, in fact, a *revolutionary* reform, that introduces an entirely new system of public education. (Chubb and Moe, 1990, p. 217)

A system of school choice would make it possible to break the iron group of powerful interest groups, unleash the positive power of competition between schools, and enable all students to aspire to academic excellence.

In order to facilitate choice, the American government should, or so Chubb and Moe argued, introduce a nationwide system of vouchers, whereby "government would provide funding directly to students in the form of these vouchers, and students would then be free to use their coupons, or vouchers, to pay for an education in the public or private school of their own choosing." It was surely time to confront the "education community," which, for the last 30 years or so, had "consistently and vehemently opposed vouchers," portraying them as "the embodiment of everything that is bad and threatening to public education" (Chubb and Moe, 1990, p. 217). At the same time, any group or organization, including a private school, that was able to meet certain "minimal criteria" could apply to the state and receive a charter to run a public school. Such groups would be granted the right to accept and educate students, and receive public money for doing so. Local districts could continue to run their own schools, but could have no authority over schools with state charters. Every Charter School would be free to set its own admissions policy, subject to the laws governing nondiscrimination, and to expel those students who refused to follow its rules. The state would hold schools accountable for meeting certain basic procedural requirements, such as providing full and accurate information to the public, but *not* for academic achievement. In a *market* system of schools, an institution's success, or otherwise, would ultimately depend on the support of the parents. In the words of Chubb and Moe: "When it comes to performance, schools are held accountable *from below*—by parents and students, who directly experience their services, and are free to choose" (Chubb and Moe, 1990, p. 225). From the above, it can be seen that in their ground-breaking book, these American academics were not merely advocating a nationwide system of vouchers; they were also putting forward the idea of Charter Schools.

In her recently published book, *The Death and Life of the Great American School System: How Testing and Choice Are Undermining Education* (2010) respected American academic Diane Ravitch argues that the works of Milton Friedman, and Chubb and Moe still exert a powerful influence on American policy-makers. She points out that the administration of George Bush Sr. (1989–1993), and the two administrations of Bill Clinton (1993–2001), advocated market reforms for the public sector, including deregulation and privatization. Professor Ravitch was herself assistant secretary of education in the Bush administration, between 1991 and 1993, and witnessed the triumph of neo-liberal, free-market views in areas such as education and health. And, in her view, the policies initiated by the Bush regime were pursued with vigor by all those working for President Bill Clinton, who shared his firm belief in a "Third Way" between the orthodox policies of the Left and those of the Right—a belief which, or so it is claimed, helped to influence the thinking of British Labour Party leader, Tony Blair. By the end of the 1990s, both Democrats and Republicans had come to look upon the public school system as obsolete, because it was in the hands of central or local government and burdened by bureaucracy. Government-run schools, said this new generation of reformers, were ineffective because they acted as a monopoly; as such, they had no incentive to do better, and they served the interests of the adults who worked in the system, not those of the students themselves. Here was a chance to "shrink the state"—hand over education to private interests and weaken the power of the teachers' unions, which were seen as simply protecting jobs and pensions while blocking effective management and innovation. And in Ravitch's view, this way of thinking, popular with both mainstream Republicans and Democrats helps to explain the bipartisan appeal of Charter Schools:

> Why shouldn't schools be managed by anyone who could supply good schools, using government funds? Free of direct government control, the schools would be innovative, hire only the best teachers, get rid of incompetent teachers, set their own pay scales, compete for students or "customers," and be judged solely by their results (test scores and also graduation rates). Good schools under private management would then proliferate; while bad schools would be closed down by market forces (the exit of disgruntled parents), or by a watchful government. Some of this new generation of reformers—mainly Republicans, but not only Republicans—imagined that the schools of the future would function without unions, allowing management to hire and fire personnel at will. With the collapse of Communism, and the triumph of market forces, in most parts of the world, it did not seem to be too much of a stretch to envision the application of the dominant market model to schooling. (Ravitch, 2010, p. 10)

Professor Ravitch admits that like many others in that era, she was attracted to the idea that the market would unleash innovation and bring greater efficiencies to the education system. But it is fair to say that she has now repudiated many of the key positions she once so strongly advocated, and believes that the undermining of public education has had all manner of harmful consequences. She now believes that it is wrong to embrace the agenda of choice and accountability whose end-result is entirely "speculative and uncertain." She concludes with a statement of her belief in "a strong and vibrant public education system" that celebrates the limitless potential of all students:

> We need to reorient our social and educational vision to see each and every child as a precious human being—a person of endless potential. Not someone rated by his or her test scores. Not defined by his or her family demographics. But as a person who is growing, developing, in need of adult guidance, in need of a challenging and liberating education, an education of possibilities and passion. (Ravitch, 2010, p. 288)

It seems clear that Australia is also a country where the comprehensive high school has an uncertain and unpredictable future, and where this type of inclusive secondary schooling has found it very difficult to attain the broad mission that its founders envisaged for it. The late 1960s and early 1970s are now considered as a high point of comprehensive high schools in Australia and of a belief in the essential virtues of centrally controlled and bureaucratically managed public education. With around 80 percent of all enrolments, state schools were responsible for the schooling of a broad cross-section of the community, and aimed to provide a curriculum that was comprehensive, inclusive and relevant.

Since that time, there has been a growing disillusionment with the very idea of comprehensive high schools being able to cater to students of *all* abilities, together with a determination, among the wealthier sections of the community, to turn to the private sector for the education of their children. Here, broadly speaking, the schools have smaller class sizes, better trained and more qualified teachers, more abundant resources, and better examination results. Able to attract the most "motivated" pupils, these schools are also very successful as stepping-stones to a university education. This means that many comprehensive schools are seen as second-class institutions for the offspring of those parents who cannot afford to send their children elsewhere. The situation has been summed up by Professor Pavla Miller of the Royal Melbourne Institute of Technology University in the following terms:

> In Australia, as in other countries, the unfinished project of making all high schools "comprehensive" is now under attack. In the 1970s, comprehensive schools were depicted as flawed but perfectible engines of democratic citizenship, neighbourliness, equality of opportunity, and effective preparation for a diversity of productive lives. Today, national governments encourage market competition between schools, provide substantial subsidies to the private education sector, are sceptical about the actual worth of public institutions, and miserly with funding them. The competition for enrolments is a serious business for government schools. In the last 15 years, many have closed, despite strong community support, because their enrolments fell beyond what education departments saw as sustainable. In turn, and often reluctantly, parents in many regions are coming to see the comprehensive schools as sort of residual institutions for those unable or unwilling to send their children elsewhere. (Miller, 2007, p. 185)

In a study of comprehensive schooling in New South Wales, Australia's largest state, Craig Campbell and Geoffrey Sherington have also traced the recent decline of the comprehensive high school, with many schools under sustained attack for low student retention rates, and poor performance in public examinations. They also note the capacity of the wealthiest and most prestigious private schools in the state to skim "talented" and "motivated" students from the state sector, which is then left providing for a disproportionately large number of children with poor language skills, fragmented family backgrounds, and a general lack of ambition. And this is a chronic situation that has been exacerbated by successive governments' fondness for market solutions to public problems in general and for discriminatory funding policies in particular. Campbell and Sherington conclude:

> The government comprehensive high school is the one secondary school in Australia that appears to be suffering the most as a result of neoliberal policy inspired changes in school funding policies. These schools, originally serving a broad cross-section of Australian families, are steadily becoming less representative. There is indeed strong evidence of middle-class "flight" from a number of these schools—which is proving very damaging.... Government funding policies are not responsive to the new pressures on comprehensive high schools, as their school populations are increasingly drawn from local populations that are subject to high unemployment, or are relatively poor and disempowered.... In the Western world, Australia now has one of the largest non-government school sectors. And despite these schools receiving public funding, they have relatively few limitations placed upon them, with regard to curriculum obligations or student acceptance or expulsion procedures. This fact produces a potentially explosive politics concerning social justice issues, as substantially free but poorly-funded government comprehensive schools find it increasingly difficult to retain those students from wealthier and academically advantaged backgrounds.... As governments search in vain for policy solutions to these very real problems, their commitment, such as it is, to public schooling is undermined by an increasingly numerous and powerful electorate committed to neoliberal versions of school choice, only made possible by federal funding of non-government schools in the first place. (Campbell and Sherington, 2006, p. 162)

In New Zealand, much of the recent education debate has centered on the significance of the 1988 Picot report. This report, with the title *Administering for Excellence: Effective Administration in Education*, was the outcome of extensive deliberations by a taskforce headed by Brian

Picot, and set up in July 1987 by the Labour prime minister and soon to be minister of education David Lange, with the task of reviewing administrative efficiency across an education system that incorporated early childhood, primary, secondary and post-compulsory education. Its wide brief included a critical scrutiny of the Department of Education's main functions, together with a reassessment of school, college, and polytechnic governing bodies, with a view to delegating responsibilities and increasing "community control" (see Openshaw, 2009, p. 3). After nine months' work, the report, published by the taskforce in April 1988, concluded that the structure of the existing education service was "a creaky, cumbersome affair." It went on:

> It is not the result of an overall plan or design, but has taken on its present shape by increments and accretion. Such a haphazard collection of administrative arrangements is simply not suited to the rapidly changing late twentieth century. In looking at the system, we have observed a number of serious weaknesses. And these can be grouped broadly under five main themes: over-centralization of decision-making; complexity; lack of information and school choice; lack of effective management practices; and feelings of "powerlessness." (Quoted in Openshaw, 2009, p. 4)

The Picot Committee had been encouraged to begin with a "blank slate" approach to educational reform; they actually came up with proposals in which the existing system of educational administration was to disappear *in its entirety*, rather than be subject to far-reaching reform. Although the report was not concerned with comprehensive secondary schooling as such, its recommendations were, in fact, to have important implications for the future structure of secondary education in New Zealand. All schools were to be transformed into autonomous, self-managing units, competing for their students in an economic marketplace characterized by consumer choice. Existing bureaucratic structures were to be replaced by "centralized auditing, and regulatory and monitoring processes across the entire education sector" (Lee, Lee, and Openshaw, 2007, p. 178). *Tomorrow's Schools*, the government's response to the Picot report's recommendations, was published without much delay and with very little consultation, in August 1988; and this document largely accepted the Picot proposals, with the legislation giving effect to the reforms coming into force on October 1, 1989.

The Picot reforms have been viewed by commentators and politicians in a number of different ways. Some have accepted the taskforce's assertion that the old education structures were both outdated and inflexible, particularly with regard to secondary schooling, and that it was necessary to encourage greater diversity as a means of providing greater choice for "educational consumers." Others have noted a sharp dichotomy between a largely imported neoliberal ideology favored by the Picot Committee, and the liberal-democratic settlement created by the first Labour government in the immediate postwar years. To this extent, it could be argued that recent New Right concepts have been an affront to "indigenous" New Zealand beliefs in community and public welfare. While others assert that welcome though the Picot reforms undoubtedly were, they have been subverted by successive governments—not least on account of a political failure to curb the power of the teacher unions. As a result, or so it is argued, powerful education bureaucracies have reemerged to wrest back the control of education from parents and local communities. All of which would seem to create the impression that the confrontation between "participatory democracy" and "New Right ideology" has ended in a draw (Openshaw, 2009, p. 184), and that "New Zealand still struggles to comprehend the full impact and meaning of mass post-primary schooling some sixty years after its inception" (Lee, Lee, and Openshaw, 2007, p. 180).

In Scandinavia, it is less apparent that governments have succumbed to neoliberal, market-driven ideologies, although, even here, there is evidence that in at least some important areas of public provision, the old order is giving way to the new. In *Education and Social Integration: Comprehensive Schooling in Europe*, a recent 2009 contribution to the debate on trends in different regions of Europe, Susanne Wiborg makes the case that the key to understanding the successful development of state comprehensive systems in Scandinavian countries is to be found in the strength of social democratic political parties and in the genuine alliances they have been able to form with liberal groups. This provides an interesting contrast with the situation in, say, England and Germany, where there has been a marked absence of strong and ideologically secure social democratic groups, and where liberal parties have been notable for their schizophrenic nature. And political factors such as these must be viewed alongside social and economic issues. Comprehensive education both reflects and enhances social cohesion. The relative homogeneity of Scandinavian societies has so far acted as a favorable factor in the promotion of "democratic" comprehensive schools; and these schools have, in turn, been seen as a convenient and necessary vehicle for creating and maintaining social and cultural cohesion (Wiborg, 2009).

It is true that in the 1990s, Sweden seemed to be making a clean break with the previous tradition of a centralized education system within a social democratic welfare society and to opt instead for neoliberal, market-oriented policies in education. During the deep recession of that decade, government policy was directed towards reducing the enormous state budget deficit, and education was one of the casualties. The non-–Social Democratic government, in office from 1991 to 1994, introduced a number of reforms in public education that delegated responsibility for public schools from central government to the local municipalities and, at the same time, experimented with a system of vouchers as a means of enhancing school choice. The period also saw an expansion in the number of "independent schools"—schools that were publicly funded but privately run.

The minority Social Democratic government did not dismantle the previous government's market-driven reforms when it regained power in 1994; but politicians insisted on viewing the independent schools as an essential part of the school system, and there was a concern to uphold egalitarian values. During the period of a later administration, from 1998 to 2002, attempts were made to mitigate some of the more negative social consequences of the privatizing measures and to preserve some of the more cohesive aspects of a comprehensive system. The independent schools were to remain under central and local government control, and through the instruments of equal financial funding, nonselective admission policies, the absence of school fees, a national curriculum, and a central inspection authority, an attempt was made to ensure "equivalence" between municipal and independent schools (Wiborg, 2009; 2010).

Conclusion

In 2004, Andy Green and Susanne Wiborg contributed a chapter on "Comprehensive Schooling and Educational Inequality" to a collection of essays entitled *Education and Democracy*, designed to celebrate the life and work of Caroline Benn, who had died at the end of 2000. In this essay, Green and Wiborg made use of the data provided by OECD Surveys to gain a clear impression of the effects of different school systems on educational inequality across countries. They concluded on the basis of this information that what the "more equal" countries had in common, which was absent in the "less equal" countries, were "the structures and processes typically associated with the radical versions of comprehensive education: nonselective schools, mixed-ability classes, late subject specialization, and measures to equalize resources between the schools" (Green and Wiborg, 2004, pp. 239–40). Heartening though these findings might be for the proponents of educational reform, they do not seem to have prevented a number of countries from introducing policies leading in quite the opposite direction. And British governments of all political complexions would appear to be much influenced by international trends. It is beyond the scope of this book to discuss the education policies of the coalition government which took office in May 2010; but it is interesting to note that the reforms of Education Secretary Michael Gove appear to have been at least partly influenced by the introduction of Free Schools in Sweden and of Charter Schools in America.

Chapter 9

Conclusion

This book has tended to concentrate on the more blatant continuities in education policy-making between the governments of Margaret Thatcher and John Major on the one hand, and those of Tony Blair and Gordon Brown on the other. But it is important to point out that in areas which had little to do with *ideology* as such, New Labour was anxious to make changes that, it was hoped, would benefit large numbers of pupils.

After an initial period, when it was deemed prudent to keep *within* Conservative spending limits, the Blair government was keen to compensate for years of low education expenditure and comparative neglect, by finding the money for the long-overdue refurbishment of many run-down school buildings, particularly in deprived, inner-city locations. New Labour's investment in technology and up-to-date resources meant that henceforth many primary and secondary school classrooms were to be strikingly well-equipped with computers, electronic whiteboards, and the like. And there was also an increase in the number of support staff in many secondary schools, ensuring that large numbers of students were now able to receive one-to-one help with their studies, or benefit from small-group provision, on a scale largely unknown in the 1980s and 1990s.

At the same time, the government's "Every Child Matters" strategy, taking its name from a green paper published in September 2003 and initially aimed at younger children, came to have an impact on the way secondary schools viewed their students. It was not enough for schools to aim for good test and examination results; they also had to look after and nourish the whole child. The Children Act of November 2004 specified *five* outcomes for all children and young people: be healthy, stay safe, enjoy and achieve, make a positive contribution to society, and achieve economic well-being. It was now expected that Ofsted inspection reports would make reference to all these five areas.

That said, the main concern of this book has been to throw light on those areas, often of a controversial nature, where New Labour has been prepared, and indeed happy, to pursue an education agenda set by its Conservative predecessors. Education was still seen as being about preparing youngsters for the position they would come to hold in the jobs market, but, more than this, it was about acknowledging that children of secondary age had widely differing "abilities" and "talents," and would benefit from being educated in different types of schools offering various specialisms. No attempt would be made to interfere with the existing hierarchy of secondary schools; indeed successive education ministers would ensure that the system would be rendered even more complicated and difficult to negotiate.

What was *not* part of New Labour's education agenda was support for the concept of the "traditional" comprehensive high school. By the time Gordon Brown's government was defeated in May 2010, the comprehensive school, where it still existed, was just *one* of nearly 20 types of secondary schools, each with its own legal status and unique if imprecise admission procedures. And this was not what the comprehensive school campaigners of the 1950s and 1960s envisaged for the future. They had thought in terms of a single unified system of fully comprehensive community schools, under local democratic control, and without private, voluntary, or selective enclaves. The Labour Party's conspicuous failure to embrace this total concept in the 1960s and 1970s, made it comparatively easy to dismantle the whole structure once disillusionment set in.

The one recent development that would have totally surprised, and indeed shocked, the early comprehensive pioneers was the increasing privatization of the education system, which has assumed so many different forms since 1979. This has been *the* dominant global trend of the recent past, meaning that we are well on the road to viewing education, like other public services, as a commodity to be bought or sold in the market-place, like all other commodities.

References

Adonis, A. and S. Pollard. (1997). *A Class Act: The Myth of Britain's Classless Society*. London: Hamish Hamilton.
ATL (Association of Teachers and Lecturers) (2010). *England's Schools: Not Open for Business*. London: ATL.
Auld, R. (1976). *William Tyndale Junior and Infants Schools Public Inquiry: A Report to the Inner London Education Authority by Robin Auld, QC*. London: Inner London Education Authority.
Baker, K. (1993). *The Turbulent Years: My Life in Politics*. London: Faber and Faber.
Ball, S. J. (1984). "Introduction: Comprehensives in Crisis." In *Comprehensive Schooling: A Reader*, edited by S. J. Ball (pp. 1–26). Lewes: Falmer Press.
———. (2007). *Education Plc: Understanding Private Sector Participation in Public Sector Education*. London: Routledge.
Barber, M. (1996). *The Learning Game: Arguments for an Education Revolution*. London: Cassell.
Beckett, F. (2007). *The Great City Academy Fraud*. London: Continuum.
Benn, C. (1992). *Keir Hardie*. London: Hutchinson.
Benn, C., and B. Simon. (1970). *Half Way There: Report on the British Comprehensive School Reform*. London: McGraw-Hill.
Benn, C., and C. Chitty. (1996). *Thirty Years On: Is Comprehensive Education Alive and Well or Struggling to Survive?* London: David Fulton.
———. (1997) *Thirty Years On: Is Comprehensive Education Alive and Well or Struggling to Survive?* Harmondsworth: Penguin Books.
Benn, M. (2011). *School Wars: The Battle for Britain's Education*. London: Verso.
Benn, T. (1987). "British Politics 1945–87: One of Four Perspectives." In *Ruling Performance: British Governments from Attlee to Thatcher*, edited by P. Hennessy and A. Seldon (pp. 301–8). Oxford: Basil Blackwell.
———. (1989). *Against the Tide: Diaries 1973–76*. London: Hutchinson.
Blackburn, F. (1954). *George Tomlinson*. London: Heinemann.
Blair, T. (1994). *Socialism*. London: The Fabian Society.
———. (2010). *A Journey*. London: Hutchinson.

Blake, R. (1966). *Disraeli*. London: Methuen.

———. (1985). *The Conservative Party from Peel to Thatcher*. London: Fontana Paperbacks.

Blishen, E. (1955). *Roaring Boys: A Schoolmaster's Agony*. London: Thames and Hudson.

———. (1957). "The Potentialities of Secondary Modern School Pupils." In *New Trends in English Education*, edited by B. Simon (pp. 74–82). London: McGibbon and Kee.

Blunkett, D. (1995). Communication with the author, July 20.

Boyle, E. (1972). "The Politics of Secondary School Reorganization: Some Reflections." *Journal of Educational Administration and History*, 4 (2), June: 28–38.

Brack, D., R. Grayson, and D. Howarth, eds. (2007). *Reinventing the State: Social Liberalism for the 21st Century*. London: Politico's.

Briggs, A. (1959). *The Age of Improvement, 1783–1867*. London: Longmans.

Brown, G. (2008). "Time for the Third Act in Public Sector Reform." *The Financial Times*, March 10.

Burt, C. (1950). "Testing Intelligence." *The Listener*, November 16.

Butler, R. A. (1950). Foreword to *One Nation: A Tory Approach to Social Problems*, edited by I. Macleod and A. Maude. London: National Union of Conservative Constitutional Associations.

Campbell, C., and G. Sherington. (2006). *The Comprehensive Public High School: Historical Perspectives*. New York: Palgrave Macmillan.

Carvel, J. (1998). "Barbed School Report Brings Battle between Advisers out into the Open." *The Guardian*, February 6.

Carvel, J., and D. Macleod. (1997). "Ambitious Plan Excites Teachers." *The Guardian*, July 8.

CASE (Campaign for State Education) (1997). *Parents and Schools*. CASE: Bulletin No. 95.

Chitty, C. (1979). "Inside the Secondary School: Problems and Prospects." In *Education and Equality*, edited by D. Rubinstein. (pp. 150–163). London: Harper and Row.

———. (1989a). *Towards A New Education System: The Victory of the New Right?* Lewes: Falmer Press.

———. (1989b). "City Technology Colleges: A Strategy for Elitism." *Forum*, 32 (3), Autumn: 8–73.

———. (1992). "The Privatization of Education." In *Education for Economic Survival: From Fordism to Post-Fordism?*, edited by P. Brown and H. Lauder (pp. 143–60). London: Routledge.

———. (1995). "Diversity and Excellence: A Recipe for Confusion." *Forum* 37 (3), Autumn: 3–93.

———. (1997a). "The White Paper: Missed Opportunities." *Forum*, 39 (3), Autumn: 71–73.

———. (1997b). "Interview with Keith Joseph." In *Radical Educational Policies and Conservative Secretaries of State*, edited by P. Ribbins and B. Sherratt. (pp. 78–86). London: Cassell.

———. (2007). *Eugenics, 'Race' and Intelligence in Education*. London: Continuum.

Chubb, J. E., and T. M. Moe. (1990). *Politics, Markets, and America's Schools*. Washington, DC: Brookings Institution Press.

Conant, J. B. (1959). *The American High School Today: A First Report to Interested Citizens*. New York: McGraw-Hill.

Cook, C. (2010 edn.). *A Short History of the Liberal Party: The Road Back to Power*. London: Palgrave Macmillan.

Corbett, A. (1969). "The Tory Educators." *New Society*, May 22.

Cox, C. B. and R. Boyson, eds. (1975). *Black Paper 1975: The Fight for Education*. London: Dent.

———, eds. (1977). *Black Paper 1977*. London: Maurice Temple Smith.

Cox, C. B. and A. E. Dyson, eds. (1969a). *Fight for Education: A Black Paper*. London: Critical Quarterly Society.

———, eds. (1969b). *Black Paper Two: The Crisis in Education*. London: Critical Quarterly Society.

———, eds. (1970). *Black Paper Three: Goodbye Mr. Short*. London: Critical Quarterly Society.

Crosland, C. A. R. (1956). *The Future of Socialism*. London: Jonathan Cape.

Crosland, S. (1982). *Tony Crosland*. London: Jonathan Cape.

Crossman, R. (1963). Introduction to W. Bagehot's *The English Constitution*. London: Fontana Paperbacks.

Dash, P. (2002). *Foreday Morning*. London: Black Amber Books.

———. (2012). "Secondary Modern School Education: An Essay in Subjugation and Repression." *Forum*, 54 (1), Spring: 103–11.

DES (Department of Education and Science) (1965). *The Organization of Secondary Education* (Circular 10/65), July 12. London: HMSO.

——— (1986). *A New Choice of School: City Technology Colleges*. London: HMSO.

——— (1987). *The National Curriculum 5–16: A Consultation Document*. London: DES.

DfE (Department for Education) (1992). *Choice and Diversity: A New Framework for Schools*. (white paper, Cm 2021). London: HMSO.

DfEE (Department for Education and Employment) (1996). *Self-Government for Schools*. (white paper, Cm 3315). London: HMSO.

——— (1997). *Excellence in Schools* (white paper, Cm 3681). London: HMSO.

——— (1998). *The Learning Age: A Renaissance for a New Britain*. London: TSO.

——— (2001) *Schools: Building on Success: Raising Standards, Promoting Diversity, Achieving Results* (green paper, Cm 5050). London: HMSO.

DfES (Department for Education and Skills) (2001). *Schools Achieving Success* (white paper, Cm 5230). London: HMSO.
——— (2002). *14–19: Extending Opportunities, Raising Standards* (consultation document, Cmnd 5342). London: HMSO.
——— (2003). *14–19: Opportunity and Excellence.* London: HMSO.
——— (2004a). *A Five Year Strategy for Children and Learners: Putting People at the Heart of Public Services.* (Cm 6272). London: TSO.
——— (2004b). *Curriculum and Qualifications Reform: Final the Working Group on 14–19 Reform.* (*The Tomlinson Report*). Nottingham: DfES Publications.
——— (2005a). *14–19 Education and Skills* (Cmnd 6746). London TSO.
——— (2005b). *Higher Standards, Better Schools for All: More Choice for Parents and Pupils* (white paper, Cm 6677).
Dunford, J. (2006). "The Grand March or Beating the Retreat?" *Forum*, 48 (1), Spring: 33–40.
Durkheim, E. (1938/1977) *The Evolution of Educational Thought: Lectures on the Formation and Development of Secondary Education in France.* London: Routledge and Kegan Paul.
Education Act 1944 (7 and 8 GEO. 6, c. 31). London: HMSO.
Edwards, T., J. Fitz, and G. Whitty. (1985). "Private Schools and Public Funding: A Comparison of Recent Policies in England and Australia." *Comparative Education*, 21 (1): 29–45.
———. (1989). *The State and Private Education: An Evaluation of the Assisted Places Scheme.* Lewes: Falmer Press.
Eggleston, J. (1965). "How Comprehensive is the Leicestershire Plan?" *New Society*, March 25.
Fenwick, I. G. K. (1976). *The Comprehensive School 1944–1970: The Politics of Secondary School Reorganization.* London: Methuen.
Ford, J. (1969). *Social Class and the Comprehensive School.* London: Routledge and Kegan Paul.
Franklin, B., and G. McCulloch. (2007) "Epilogue—The Future of the Comprehensive High School." In *The Death of the Comprehensive High School? Historical, Contemporary, and Comparative Perspectives*, edited by B. Franklin and G. McCulloch (pp. 201–4). New York: Palgrave Macmillan.
Friedman, M. (1955). "The Role of Government in Education." In *Economics and the Public Interest*, edited by Robert A. Solo (pp. 123–44). New Brunswick, NJ: Rutgers University Press.
Gamble, A. (1988). *The Free Economy and the Strong State: The Politics of Thatcherism.* London: Macmillan.
Garner, R. (2004). "Should These People Be Running State Schools?" *The Independent*, July 8.

———. (2008). "Lord's Prayer: Andrew Adonis on Why He Still Has Faith in Academies." *The Independent*, May 1.
Giddens, A. (1994). *Beyond Left and Right*. Cambridge: Polity Press.
———. (1998a). *The Third Way: The Renewal of Social Democracy*. Cambridge: Polity Press.
———. (1998b). "The Future of the Welfare State." In *Is There a Third Way?*, edited by M. Novak. London: Institute of Economic Affairs.
Gilmour, I., and M. Garnett. (1997). *Whatever Happened to the Tories: The Conservative Party since 1945*. London: Fourth Estate.
Grayson, R. (2009). "Social Liberalism." In *The Political Thought of the Liberals and Liberal Democrats Since 1945*, edited by K. Hickson (pp. 48–64). Manchester: Manchester University Press.
Green, A., and S. Wiborg. (2004). "Comprehensive Schooling and Educational Inequality an Historical Perspective." In *Education and Democracy A Tribute to Caroline Benn*, edited by M. Benn and C. Chitty (pp. 217–42). London: Continuum.
Griggs, C. (1985). *Private Education in Britain*. Lewes: Falmer Press.
———. (1989). "The New Right and English Secondary Education." In *The Changing Secondary School*, edited by R. Lowe (pp. 99–128). Lewes: Falmer Press.
Hall, S. (2011). "The Neoliberal Revolution." *Soundings*, Issue 48, Summer: 9–27.
Hall, S., and D. Massey. (2010). "Interpreting the Crisis." *Soundings*, Issue 44, Spring: 57–71.
Halsey, A. H. (1965). "Education and Equality." *New Society*, June 17.
Hargreaves, D. H. (1982). *The Challenge for the Comprehensive School: Culture, Curriculum and Community*. London: Routledge and Kegan Paul.
Hatcher, R. (1997). "New Labour and Comprehensive Education." *Forum* 39 (1), Spring: 6–9.
———. (2001). "Privatization and Schooling." In *Promoting Comprehensive Education in the 21st Century*, edited by C. Chitty and B. Simon (pp. 63–73). Stoke on Trent: Trentham Books.
Hattersley, R. (1995). "Labour's Big, Bad Idea." *The Independent*, June 22.
———. (1997a). "Battle of the Lip-Readers." *The Guardian*, November 28.
———. (1997b). *Fifty Years On: A Prejudiced History of Britain since the War*. London: Little, Brown and Company.
Hattersley, R. and K. Hickson. (2011). "In Praise of Social Democracy." *The Political Quarterly*, 83 (1): 5–12.
Hennessy, P. (2012). *Distilling the Frenzy: Writing the History of One's Own Time*. London: Biteback Publishing.
Hickson, K., ed. (2009). *The Political Thought of the Liberals and Liberal Democrats since 1945*. Manchester: Manchester University Press.

Hobsbawm, E. (1984). *Worlds of Labour: Further Studies in the History of Labour.* London: Weidenfeld and Nicolson.
Hughes, C. (1988). "Privatizer on Parade: A Profile of Oliver Letwin." *The Independent,* June 6.
Hugill, B. (1994). "Labour U-turn on School League Tables." *The Observer,* October 30.
Hutton, W. (1995). *The State We're in.* London: Jonathan Cape.
Jones, G. (1994). "Blair Warns Left to Shed Dogmas." *The Daily Telegraph,* July 26.
Joseph, K. (1976). *Stranded on the Middle Ground? Reflections on Circumstances and Policies.* London: Centre for Policy Studies.
Katz, I. (1994). "The Rethink-Tank Man." *The Guardian,* October 17.
Kavanagh, D. (1987). *Thatcherism and British Politics: The End of Consensus.* Oxford: Oxford University Press.
Kerckhoff, A., K. Fogelman, D. Crook, and D. Reeder. (1996). *Going Comprehensive in England and Wales: A Study of Uneven Change.* London: Woburn Press.
Knight, C. (1990). *The Making of Tory Education Policy in Post-war Britain, 1950–1986.* Lewes: Falmer Press.
Kogan, M. (1971). *The Politics of Education: Edward Boyle and Anthony Crosland in Conversation with Maurice Kogan.* Harmondsworth: Penguin.
Labour Party (1993). *Opening Doors to a Learning Society* (A Consultative Green Paper on Education). London: Labour Party.
——— (1994). *Opening Doors to a Learning Society* (A Policy Statement on Education). London: Labour Party.
——— (1995). *Diversity and Excellence: A New Partnership for Schools.* London: Labour Party.
——— (1997). *Because Britain Deserves Better.* London: Labour Party.
——— (2005) *Britain Forward Not Back.* London: Labour Party.
Lawton, D. (1980). *The Politics of the School Curriculum.* London: Routledge and Kegan Paul.
———. (1994). *The Tory Mind on Education, 1979–94.* London: Falmer.
———. (2005). *Education and Labour Party Ideologies: 1900–2001 and beyond.* London: RoutledgeFalmer.
Lee, G., H. Lee, and R. Openshaw. (2007). "The Comprehensive Ideal in New Zealand:Challenges and Prospects." In *The Death of the Comprehensive High School? Historical, Contemporary, and Comparative Perspectives,* edited by B. Franklin and G. McCulloch (pp. 169–84). New York: Palgrave Macmillan.
LSI (Local Schools Information) (1992). *Opting Out: 1988–1992: An Analysis.* London: LSI.
Macintyre, D. (1994). "Young Academic Given Key Role of Developing Policy for Leader." *The Independent,* July 23.

Mandelson, P., and R. Liddle. (1996). *The Blair Revolution. Can New Labour Deliver?* London: Faber and Faber.

Mansell, W. (2005). "Playing Politics with Our Exams." *The Times Educational Supplement*, February 25.

Marquand, D. (1977). *Ramsay MacDonald*. London: Jonathan Cape.

———. (1988). *The Unprincipled Society: New Demands and Old Politics*. London: Jonathan Cape.

Marshall, P., and D. Laws, eds. (2004). *The Orange Book: Reclaiming Liberalism*. London: Profile Books.

McCulloch, G. (1998). *Failing the Ordinary Child? The Theory and Practice of Working-Class Secondary Education*. Buckingham: Open University Press.

Miliband, D. (2004). Interview with the author, August 24.

———. (2012). "The Dead End of the Big State." *New Statesman*, February 6: 22–25.

Miliband, R. (1969). *The State in Capitalist Society*. London: Weidenfeld and Nicolson.

Millar, F. (2005). "Nowhere in the Manifesto." *The Guardian*, November 15.

Miller, P. (2007). "'My Parents Came Here with Nothing and They Wanted Us to Achieve': Italian Australians and School Success." In *The Death of the Comprehensive High School? Historical, Contemporary, and Comparative Perspectives*, edited by B. Franklin and G. McCulloch (pp. 185–198). New York: Palgrave Macmillan.

Ministry of Education (1951). *Education, 1900–1950* (Cm. 8244). London: HMSO.

——— (1963). *Half Our Future (The Newsom Report)*. London: HMSO.

Monks, T. G. (1968). *Comprehensive Education in England and Wales: A Survey of Schools and their Organization*. National Foundation for Educational Research in England and Wales. Research Reports: Second Series, No. 6. Slough: NFER.

Morgan, J., ed. (1981). *The Backbench Diaries of Richard Crossman*. London: Hamish Hamilton and Jonathan Cape.

Morgan, K. O. (1981). *Rebirth of a Nation: Wales, 1880–1980*. Oxford and Cardiff: Clarendon Press; University of Wales Press.

———. (1984). *Labour in Power: 1945–1951*. Oxford: Clarendon Press.

Morris, E. (2002a). *Transforming Secondary Education: The Middle Years*. London: DfES.

———. (2002b). "Why Comprehensives Must Change." *The Observer*, June 23.

Mortimore, P. (1998). "A Big Step Backward." *Education Guardian*, March 24.

Mountfield, A. (1991). *State Schools: A Suitable Case for Charity?* London: Directory of Social Change Publications.

Nelson, F. (2007). "We Should Have Been Bolder: Interview with Andrew Adonis," *The Spectator*, January 24: 3.

Novak, M., ed. (1998). *Is there a Third Way?* London: Institute of Economic Affairs.

Openshaw, R. (2009). *Reforming New Zealand Secondary Education: The Picot Report and the Road to Radical Reform.* New York: Palgrave Macmillan.

Parkinson, M. (1970). *The Labour Party and the Organization of Secondary Education, 1918–1965.* London: Routledge and Kegan Paul.

Patten, J. (1992) "Who's Afraid of the 'S' word?" *New Statesman and Society*, July 17: 20–21.

Pedley, R. R. (1969). "Comprehensive Disaster." In *Fight for Education: A Black Paper*, edited by C. B. Cox and A. E. Dyson (pp. 45–48). London: Critical Quarterly Society.

Power, S. and G. Whitty. (1999). "New Labour's Education Policy: First, Second or Third Way." *Journal of Education Policy*, 14 (5): 535–46.

Pring, R. (1983). *Privatization in Education.* London: RICE (Right to a Comprehensive Education).

———. (1986). "Privatization of Education." In *Education and Social Class*, edited by R. Rogers (pp. 65–82). Lewes: Falmer Press.

———. (1987a). "Privatization in Education." *Journal of Education Policy*, 2 (4): 289–99.

———. (1987b). "Free… to Those Who Contribute." *The Times Educational Supplement*, October 23.

Pugh, M. (2005). *"Hurrah for the Blackshirts!" Fascists and Fascism in Britain between the Wars.* London: Jonathan Cape.

Ravitch, D. (2010). *The Death and Life of the Great American School System: How Testing and Choice are undermining Education.* New York: Basic Books.

Rentoul, J. (2001). *Tony Blair: Prime Minister.* London: Warner Books.

Rogers, M., and F. Migniulo. (2007). *A New Direction: A Review of the School Academies Programme.* London: TUC.

Rubinstein, D., and B. Simon. (1973). *The Evolution of the Comprehensive School, 1926–1972.* London: Routledge and Kegan Paul.

SCAA (School Curriculum and Assessment Authority) (1994). *The National Curriculum and its Assessment.* Final Report. London: SCAA.

Searle, C. (2001). *An Exclusive Education: Race, Class and Exclusion in British Schools.* London: Lawrence and Wishart.

Seldon, A. (1986). *The Riddle of the Voucher.* London: Institute of Economic Affairs.

———. (2004). *Blair.* London: Free Press.

Sexton, S. (1988). "No Nationalized Curriculum." *The Times*, May 9.

———. (1995). Interview with the author. November 24.

Simon, B. (1955). *The Common Secondary School.* London: Lawrence and Wishart.

———. (1960). *Studies in the History of Education, 1780–1870*. London: Lawrence and Wishart.

———. (1974). *The Politics of Educational Reform, 1920–1940*. London: Lawrence and Wishart.

———. (1994). *The State and Educational Change: Essays in the History of Education and Pedagogy*. London: Lawrence and Wishart.

Stevenson, H. (1996). "Policy, Practice and Post-Fordism: What Future for Education?" *Forum* 38 (1), Spring: 7–9.

Tawney, R. H. (1922). *Secondary Education for All: A Policy for Labour*. London: George Allen and Unwin.

Taylor, A. (1994). "Schools CAN Make a Difference." *Forum* 36 (1), Spring: 4–5.

Taylor, W. (1963). *The Secondary Modern School*. London: Faber and Faber.

Timms, S. (2001) "Grammar and Non-selective Schools to Work Together in £5m Boost." Press Release, December 7.

Tomlinson, S. (2nd edn. 2005). *Education in a Post-welfare Society*. Maidenhead: Open University Press.

Tomlinson, S. (2012). Interview with the author, April 25.

Vernon, B. D. (1982). *Ellen Wilkinson, 1891–1947*. London: Croom Helm.

Ward, L. (1997). "Government to Have Its Hand in Every School." *The Independent*, July 8.

Webb, S. (1908). "Secondary Education." In *A Century of Education*, edited by H. B. Binns (pp. 284–96). London: Dent.

Whitfield, D. (2001). *Public Services or Corporate Welfare?* London: Pluto Press.

Wiborg, S. (2009). *Education and Social Integration: Comprehensive Schooling in Europe*. New York: Palgrave Macmillan.

———. (2010). "Learning Lessons from the Swedish Model." *Forum*, 52 (3), Autumn: 279–84.

Wilkinson, E. (1939). *The Town That Was Murdered: The Life-Story of Jarrow*. London: Victor Gollancz.

Worcester, R. (1999). *Explaining Labour's Landslide*. London: Politico's.

Young, H. (1989). *One of Us: A Biography of Margaret Thatcher* London: Macmillan.

Index

3Es Enterprises Ltd, 118
11-plus selection, 29, 37, 40–41,
　44–45, 47, 55, 80, 90–91, 102–3
14–19 curriculum, 5, 133, 138, 141,
　143, 145, 147

A Levels, 142–49
Able, Graham, 127
Academies Programme, 5, 66, 92, 96,
　102, 113, 122–26, 128
Admissions Code of Practice, 102, 104
Adonis, Andrew, 66
Assisted Places Scheme, 60, 81, 82, 109
Association of Language Learning
　(ALL), 140
Attlee, Clement, 13, 25, 35, 43
Australian schools, 160–62

Bagehot, Walter, 24
Baker, Kenneth, 5, 27, 55, 113–14,
　122, 129–31, 133, 136, 141
Balls, Ed, 147–48
Barber, Michael, 71, 75–76, 85
BAT Industries, 115
Because Britain Deserves Better, 80
Beckett, Margaret, 60
Benn, Caroline, 22, 27, 32, 47–48, 50,
　126, 128, 151–53, 155, 165
Benn, Tony, 8
Bentham, Jeremy, 64
Bevan, Aneurin, 19
Beveridge, William, 18–19
Beveridge Report, 19

Beyond Left and Right (Giddens), 2
Black, George, 120
black papers, 50–53, 110
Blackburn, Fred, 36
Blackpool conference (1994), 62, 70
Blackpool conference (2002), 99
Blair, Tony
　1997 White Paper, 82, 87–88
　2005 White Paper, 101, 103
　Academies Program and, 123–26
　Assisted Places Scheme and, 109
　Because Britain Deserves Better and,
　　79–80
　Blair Project, 60–65
　Clinton and, 2, 159
　comprehensive schools and, 90,
　　93–94, 96, 99
　election as leader of Labour, 1, 4, 28,
　　60, 76–77
　Excellence in Schools and, 82
　expenditures on education, 167
　intellectual preparations for
　　government and, 75–76
　national curriculum and, 136
　privatization and, 116–19
　renaming of Labour Party, 2
　secondary education and, 82,
　　87–88, 90, 105
　selection and, 65–68, 70–72, 74
　Third Way and, 159
　Tomlinson Report and, 144–45, 147
*Blair Revolution: Can New Labour
　Deliver?* (Barber), 75, 87

Blishen, Edward, 37–38, 40
Blunkett, David, 9, 29, 70–74, 83, 90, 92–96, 122, 124, 153
Board of Education Act (1899), 26
Boyle, Edward, 42, 48, 51–52
Boyson, Rhodes, 52–53, 110
Breakfast with Frost, 74, 90
Brighouse, Tim, 85
Brown, Gordon, 1, 60, 125, 126–28, 137, 147–49, 167–68
Burt, Cyril, 47
Bush, George H.W., 159
Bush, George W., 74
Butler, R.A., 13, 25
"Butskellism," 25

Callaghan, James, 53–54
Cameron, David, 7, 9, 19
Campaign for State Education (CASE), 87, 91
Campbell, Alastair, 2, 62, 94, 99
Campbell, Craig, 161–62
Campbell-Bannerman, Henry, 16, 22, 79
Carlisle, Mark, 109, 111
Carvel, J., 85, 87
Chamberlain, Joseph, 20
Charter Schools, 158–60, 169
Children Act (2004), 168
Choice and Diversity: A New Framework for Schools (Patten), 59
Chubb, John E., 157–59
church schools, 60, 72, 81, 86, 95, 127, 157
Circular 10/65, 27, 42–43, 46–48, 50–51
City Technology Colleges (CTCs), 28, 55, 57, 60, 72, 113–14, 118, 122, 132
Clarke, Charles, 100–101
Clarke, Kenneth, 133, 141–42, 144
Class Act: The Myth of Britain's Classless Society, A (Adonis), 66
Clause Four of Labour Party's 1918 Constitution, 23, 62, 65

Clegg, Nick, 7
Clinton, Bill, 2, 63, 159
Cole, G.D.H., 23
Confederation of British Industry (CBI), 125, 147
Conservative Enemy, The (Crosland), 43
Conservative Party
  1988 Education Reform Act, 1
  A Levels and, 148–49
  Academies Programme and, 123, 125
  Blair and, 57–60, 70, 72, 82
  Circular 10/65 and, 42–43, 46, 48, 51–54
  Education and Inspections Bill, 104
  evolution of, 7–9
  history, 9–16
  Labour and, 22, 57–60, 79–82, 114, 127, 153
  Liberals and, 17, 19
  National Curriculum and, 129–31, 133–36
  privatization and, 54–55, 110–11, 113–15
  public education and, 25, 27–28, 51–55, 127, 153, 167–68
  reactions to, 54–55
  Third Way and, 2
  see also City Technology Colleges (CTCs); Major, John; Thatcher, Margaret
continuity, 10, 68–69, 82
Cook, Chris, 17
Crosland, Anthony, 43–44, 46, 49
Crossman, Richard, 24, 37

Dearing, Ron, 134–36, 138
Demos, 137
Department for Education and Employment (DfEE), 84–86, 118
Department for Education and Science (DES), 43–44, 50, 54, 132–33
Department for Education and Skills (DfES), 96, 100, 123, 140–42

Department of Health and Social
    Security (DHSS), 14, 110
deregulation, 55, 111, 157, 159
Disraeli, Benjamin, 8, 11–13, 17
*Distilling the Frenzy: Writing the
    History of One's Own Times*
    (Hennessy), 3
*Diversity and Excellence: A New
    Partnership for Schools*, 72–73, 85
Dunford, John, 99, 103, 146, 148

Ede, J. Chuter, 35
Education Action Zones (EAZs),
    81–82, 84, 96–97, 117
Education Acts
    1902, 32
    1944, 13, 26–27, 34–39, 128
    1980, 109
    1992, 82, 116
    1998, 82–90
    2002, 96
    2006, 101–5
Education and Inspections Bill, 104–5
Education and Skills Bill, 122
Education in a Post-welfare Society
    (Tomlinson), 29
Education Reform Acts
    1832, 9–10, 17
    1867, 17
    1988, 5, 27, 57, 70, 122, 130, 132
engineering, 95–96, 145, 147–48
English (language) education, 130–31,
    136, 139, 141, 145, 149
"equality of opportunity," 4, 59, 62,
    83, 98–99, 105, 155–56, 161
"Every Child Matters" strategy, 167
Excellence in Cities (EiC) Programme,
    97, 118
Excellence in Schools, 75, 82, 86–89,
    96, 117
Exchange Rate Mechanism, 79
Explaining Labour's Landslide
    (Worcester), 64
Eysenck, Hans, 47

Fabian Society, 32, 49, 61–62, 64
Fenwick, Keith, 36–37, 42
Fight for Education (Pedley), 50–52
*Five Year Strategy for Children and
    Learners*, 100, 123
Ford, Julienne, 51
Franklin, Barry, 153–54, 156
Friends of the Education Voucher
    Experiment in Representative
    Regions (FEVER), 111
Frost, David, 74, 90
Future of Socialism, The (Crosland),
    43, 49

Gaitskell, Hugh, 25, 34, 39
Gamble, Andrew, 3, 15–16, 117
Garner, Richard, 123–24, 127
GCSE, 92, 97, 134, 139, 142–49
General Agreement on Trade and
    Services (GATS), 121–22
General Certificate of Education
    (GCE), 41
General Education Management
    Systems (GEMS), 103, 128
Giddens, Anthony, 2, 111, 116–17
Gove, Michael, 138
Grant-Maintained (GM) schools, 28, 86
Grayson, Richard, 18–19
Green, Andy, 165–66
green papers, 67–68, 92, 94, 96,
    138–41, 167
Griggs, Clive, 110

Half Way There (Benn and Halsey),
    50, 151, 155
Hall, Stuart, 24, 63
Halsey, A.H., 49
Hardie, Keir, 22, 31–32
Hargreaves, David, 39–40
Harman, Harriet, 71
Hart, David, 87
Hatcher, Richard, 73, 120–22
Hattersley, Roy, 43, 64, 73–74
Hawkins, Nick, 153

Healey, Denis, 27
Heath, Edward, 8, 13–14, 110
Hennessy, Peter, 3
Hickson, Kevin, 19, 64
HMIs (Her Majesty's Inspectors), 108, 116
Hobsbawm, Eric, 3
Hutton, Will, 76

Institute for Public Policy Research (IPPR), 71
Institute of Economic Affairs (IEA), 110, 113, 116, 131
International Monetary Fund (IMF), 27

Jenkins, Roy, 8
Jones, George, 69
Joseph, Keith, 16, 54, 109–11, 113–15, 132
Journey, A (Blair), 2, 61, 65

Katz, Ian, 71
Kelly, Ruth, 101, 103, 145–46
Key Stage Four, 5, 133–36, 138–42, 149
Key Stage Three, 131, 135–38
Key Stage Two, 140
Keynesian Social Democracy, 4, 16, 24–27, 111
Kogan, Maurice, 43–44

Labour Party
  1944 Education Act and aftermath, 34–42
  1997 landslide victory, 64, 79
  1997 white paper/1998 Education Act, 82–90
  2005 white paper/2006 Education Act, 101–5
  changes to secondary curriculum, 136–42
  Circular 10/65 and, 42–54
  common schooling debate and, 31–34
  Conservative Party and, 22, 54–55, 57–60, 79–82, 114, 127, 153
  New Labour manifesto, 79–82
  origins and principles of, 20–24
  privatization and, 109, 116–18, 127–28, 151, 168
  reaction to Conservative agenda, 54–55
  selection and, 65–74, 90–101
  socialism and, 21–25, 43, 49, 52, 58, 66
  Thatcher and, 1, 16, 53–55, 116–17, 167
  Tomlinson Report and, 143, 148
  see also Blair, Tony; Academies Programme
Lange, David, 163
Lawton, Denis, 11, 36, 69
LEA schools, 44, 60, 72, 84–86, 109, 112, 118, 141
Learning and Skills Councils (LSCs), 141
Learning Game: Arguments for an Education Revolution (Barber), 75–76
Leicestershire Plan, 46
Letwin, Oliver, 114
Liberal Democratic Party, 7, 9, 16, 19, 124
Liberal Party, 8, 16–20, 22, 25, 79, 104
Liddle, Roger, 75, 87
Lloyd George, David, 17, 19, 37
Local Schools Information (LSI), 57
Lord Alexander, 109

MacDonald, Ramsay, 3
Macintyre, Donald, 71
Macleod, D., 87
Major, John, 4, 54, 57, 79, 115–16, 119, 133–34, 149, 167
Major Contractors Group (MCG), 120
Mandelson, Peter, 75, 87
Marquand, David, 3, 25, 51
Massey, Doreen, 24
mathematics, 96, 101, 130–32, 134, 136, 139, 141, 145, 149

Maud, John, 26
McAvoy, Doug, 87, 99
McCulloch, Gary, 40–41, 153–54, 156
McQuoid, Nigel, 125
Miliband, David, 64–65, 71, 75, 82
Miliband, Ed, 9
Miliband, Ralph, 24, 71
Millar, Fiona, 103
Miller, Pavla, 161
Millett, Anthea, 82
Moe, Terry, 157–59
Morris, Estelle, 89, 91, 96, 98–99, 118, 137–38
Mortimore, Peter, 89

National Confederation of Parent Teacher Associations (NCPTA), 108
National Council for Educational Standards (NCES), 53
National Curriculum, 5, 28, 58–59, 114, 129–49, 165
National Foundation for Educational Research (NFER), 50
National Health Service, 19
National Union of Teachers, 36, 68, 70, 87, 92, 99, 103
Nelson, Fraser, 67
New Right, 15–16, 116, 129, 164
New Zealand schools, 5, 162–64
Novak, Michael, 116

Office for Standards in Education (Ofsted), 82, 84, 88, 116, 168
Opening Doors to a Learning Society (Taylor), 67–68
Orange Book: Reclaiming Liberalism (Marshall and Laws, 19

"parity of esteem," 38, 59, 146
Parkinson, Michael, 33, 36
Patten, John, 58–59
Pedley, R.R., 50–51
Peel, Robert, 7, 9–11, 17–18

Pengam Grammar School, 37
Picot report, 162–64
Power, Sally, 116
Prescott, John, 60
Pring, Richard, 107–9
Private Finance Initiative (PFI), 5, 119–21
privatization, 14, 23, 55, 63, 93, 103
  Academies Programme, 122–27
  Clinton and, 159
  early initiatives, 110–16
  International Privatization Congress, 154
  New Labour's approach to, 116–18, 151, 168
  New Labour's stance on, 127–28
  private finance initiative, 118–21
  Reagan and, 157
  Social Democrats and, 165
  types of, 107–9
Public Private Partnerships (PPPs), 119–21

Qualifications and Curriculum Agency (QCA), 82
Queen Victoria, 17

Ravitch, Diane, 159–60
"Read my lips," 73–74
Reagan, Ronald, 157
reforms
  long-term, 127, 141–42
  short-term, 141
Reid, John, 9
Reinventing the State (Brack, Grayson, and Howarth), 19
religious education, 131, 133, 135–36, 140–42
religious schools
  see church schools
Ripon Grammar School, 91
Roaring Boys: A Schoolmaster's Agony (Blishen), 40
Rubinstein, D., 35, 37

Russell Group, 143
Ryan, Conor, 71

Scandinavian schools, 5, 164
School Curriculum and Assessment Authority (SCAA), 134–35
sciences, 28, 41, 95–96, 101, 130–32, 134–36, 139, 141, 145, 147, 149
  see also Department for Education and Science (DES)
Secondary Education for All: A Policy for Labour (Tawney), 32
Self-Government for Schools (Shephard), 59–60
Seldon, Anthony, 68, 76, 113, 127
Shephard, Gillian, 59, 115
Sherington, Geoffrey, 161–62
Sherman, Alfred, 14, 111, 115
Shinwell, Emanuel, 38–39
Short History of the Liberal Party (Cook), 17
Simon, Brian, 35, 37, 41, 47–48, 50, 151–53, 155
Smith, John, 28, 60–61, 64, 67, 79
Smithers, Rebecca, 143
Snow, C.P., 42
Social Democratic Party, 16, 19–20, 23–25, 165
Social Market Foundation (SMF), 122
social mixing, 49
Socialism
  Blair and, 61–63
  Crosland on, 43, 49
  ethical, 62
  Labour Party and, 21–25, 43, 49, 52, 58, 66
  public education and, 31, 33, 37, 153
  Third Way and, 116
specialist schools, 60, 72, 84, 87–91, 93, 95–102, 104, 115, 122, 125, 168
specialization, 32, 58–60, 90, 95, 145, 152, 166
Standards Task Force (STF), 85

State We're In, The (Barber), 76
Stewart, Michael, 43
Straw, Jack, 55, 67, 69, 114
Sweden, 155–56

Tallis, Bill, 120
Tate, Nicholas, 82
Tawney, R.H., 23, 32–33, 66
Taylor, Ann, 67–70
Taylor, William, 38
Teacher Training Agency (TTA), 82
testing, 40–41, 44, 48, 58, 70, 74, 89, 134, 158–60
Thatcher, Margaret
  1988 Education Reform Act and, 27, 57
  Blair and, 116–17
  Conservative Party and, 8, 10–11, 13–14
  CTC Project and, 113
  Labour and, 1, 16, 53–55, 116–17, 167
  national curriculum and, 4, 129–30, 132
  Pring and, 108–9
  privatization and, 23, 55, 110–11, 113, 115–17, 154
Third Way, 2, 63, 116–17, 159
Tomlinson, George, 26, 36–37
Tomlinson, Mike, 141–42
Tomlinson, Sally, 29, 55, 69
Tomlinson Report, 5, 142–49
Tory Party, 9–14, 17–18, 44, 62, 65, 146
Turbulent Years: My Life in Politics (Baker), 130

United Learning Trust (ULT), 127–28
United States, 16, 24, 31, 152, 155–56

Vardy, Peter, 124
Vernon, Betty, 36

vouchers, 52, 54, 110–13, 157–59, 165

Webb, Sydney, 32, 66
Whig Party, 17–18
White Papers
    1997, 82–90, 96
    2005, 101–5, 146
Whitty, Geoff, 116, 154–55
Wiborg, Susanne, 165–66
Wilby, Peter, 28
Wilkinson, Ellen, 35–36
William Tyndale Junior School, 53
Wilson, Harold, 39, 43, 47, 51
Woodhead, Chris, 82, 85, 128
Worcester, Robert, 64
World Bank, 122
World Trade Organization, 122

GPSR Compliance

The European Union's (EU) General Product Safety Regulation (GPSR) is a set of rules that requires consumer products to be safe and our obligations to ensure this.

If you have any concerns about our products, you can contact us on

ProductSafety@springernature.com

In case Publisher is established outside the EU, the EU authorized representative is:

Springer Nature Customer Service Center GmbH
Europaplatz 3
69115 Heidelberg, Germany

www.ingramcontent.com/pod-product-compliance
Lightning Source LLC
LaVergne TN
LVHW011825060526
838200LV00053B/3907